Praise for
On the Job

"This book is loaded with *sound* advice on this most important topic—your career."

JEFF TAYLOR,
CEO, Monster.com

"This is a sensational book that redefines the landscape of work and brings it into a real twenty-first century perspective."

SHERE HITE,
author of *Sex and Business: Ethics of
Sexuality in Business and the Workplace*

"Expect to hear the truth from Stephen Viscusi, a top executive recruiter, who reveals the hidden process in *On the Job.*"

ADELE M. SCHEELE,
author of *Jumpstart Your Career in College*

STEPHEN VISCUSI

On the Job

HOW TO MAKE IT IN THE REAL WORLD OF WORK

A Lark Production

 THREE RIVERS PRESS • NEW YORK

Published by Three Rivers Press, New York, New York.
Member of the Crown Publishing Group.

Random House, Inc. New York, Toronto, London, Sydney, Auckland
www.randomhouse.com

THREE RIVERS PRESS is a registered trademark and the Three Rivers Press colophon is a trademark of Random House, Inc.

Printed in the United States of America

Design by Barbara Sturman

Library of Congress Cataloging-in-Publication Data
Viscusi, Stephen.
　　On the job : how to make it in the real world of work / Stephen Viscusi.
　　　　p.　cm.
　　1. Work—Psychological aspects.　I. Title: How to make it in the real world of work.　II. Title.
　BF481.V57　2001
　158.7—dc21　　　00-045573

ISBN 0-609-80686-6 (pbk.)

10 9 8 7 6 5 4 3 2 1

First Edition

TO MY SISTER, LAURA,

whose love, support, and friendship have seen me through,

AND TO CASEY MCNAMARA,

whose constant support has always helped me on the job.

CONTENTS

On the Job

The First Day of My Career

REMEMBER THE FIRST DAY OF YOUR FIRST JOB? As you got ready for work and arrived at the gas station, restaurant, town pool, department store, or wherever this job took you, chances are you weren't thinking "Today is the beginning of my lifelong career." You probably were preoccupied with far more immediate, practical concerns: What will my coworkers be like? Will I understand everything I'm supposed to do? Am I wearing the right clothes? Will I last till the end of the day?

The careerist perspective won't in itself help a person deal with the strange and wonderful world of the workplace. Our productive lives comprise days of work, not days of career. That's why I focus on the day-to-day reality of work and jobs—not the lofty vistas of a "career"—in this book. I write about working: what it's really like, how to cope with it, and how to succeed at it with your sanity, humor, and integrity intact.

I've seen too many people with rigid career goals blow it when facing an especially thorny work situation; a few incidents will demolish their castle in the sand. Flexibility and spontaneous response, not adherence to a preconceived five-year plan, are the very qualities you need if you want to field the situations life tosses you.

I'm certainly not suggesting that a "job" is more important than a "career." Nor are they mutually exclusive. On the contrary, virtually all of the candidates my headhunting firm has placed over the years who master workplace dynamics have superb careers. It's inevitable: Mastery on the job entails both working well and cultivating the key relationships that advance a person's career.

A few lucky souls possess an uncanny intuitive knowledge of how work works. But not everyone grasps all the nuances, especially if they're new to the workforce. I'll never forget my own first job. But before I tell you about it, you need some background. My family lived in Armonk, New York, an affluent Westchester County suburb that houses the world headquarters of IBM—the Microsoft of the sixties and seventies. Many of my schoolmates had lived in exotic places such as Japan, Bombay, or the Philippines, and everyone knew the relative pecking order at IBM—who bossed whom. They dwelt primarily in exclusive neighborhoods called Windmill Farms, Whippoorwill, and Usonia, and those kids with really "important" dads eventually moved next door, to Greenwich, Connecticut. None of their mothers worked outside the home.

But my family was another story. My father worked at the county newspaper as a pressman, pouring the lead that was the chief ingredient in newsprint back then. And my mother sold children's shoes at R.H. Macy's department store. Dad got the job the day after his army discharge, and Mom got hers immediately after high school graduation. They both worked the same jobs until they were forced to retire for health reasons—my father at sixty-two and my mother at sixty. They didn't even consider looking for other positions elsewhere.

So, as a blue-collar kid in a white-collar town, I absorbed my parents' old-fashioned concept of success: work hard, show up on time, be polite and respectful.

Working papers in my fourteen-year-old hand, I quickly found my first job at the local drugstore. It was the only drugstore in town, and everyone went there. I was very excited, thinking it would be great fun to work the cash register. I thought it would be cool ringing things up and talking to people. I got very dressed up, as if I were a real professional—and then my mother drove me to the store. I handed my working papers to Johnny D, the owner. He began to show me around the drugstore, and we walked right past the cash register and down a long stairway to the stockroom. When I arrived each day after school around 3:30, I was to replenish the shelves with sanitary napkins, shampoos, laxatives, and a few other choice items that apparently sold the fastest.

I was acutely overdressed for the lowly job and a hundred years younger than the pharmacist, who looked like he was doing a little drug sampling; a fifty-year-old counterman; and the bookkeeper, Mrs. Brown. I really wasn't sure I would make it through the day. I just wanted to run that register. What would people say if they saw me loading up shelves of Kotex all afternoon! Could I survive the embarrassment? But I remembered my friends always seemed to have things my family couldn't afford. If I wanted spending money, I knew I needed to make that job work. And work it did.

I stayed at that job for two years, eventually even getting to work the cash register. Then I went to work at a local furniture store. Little did I know, at sixteen, that my first day at the Modern Furniture Barn (The Yellow Barn) in Armonk, New York, would be the beginning of a twenty-year career in the furniture industry.

After paying my way through college by working at the store on weekends, I stayed on after graduation to create an office furniture division. I could easily have followed my parents' path and stayed at that job forever. But the white-collar town had rubbed off on this blue-collar kid. It had made me ambitious to shoot higher, for money and everything that comes with it.

Nevertheless, if not for a distasteful event that occurred to me at the Barn, I might have stuck around there longer, and my career might not have taken the turn it did.

After five years at the company, where I had made an immense contribution, I asked the owner to be sent on the annual furniture-buying trip to Scandinavia—a privilege I'd certainly earned. He seemed more than willing to send me. But the store's general manager, who had always felt threatened by my role at the company, ultimately prevailed upon the owner to veto the request.

As soon as that happened, I thought the unthinkable: I had to leave the job. Since I had recently retained a headhunter to hire people for me, the connections were in place. In fact, the only hard part was telling my family, who were as appalled as if I had been fired.

I quickly found an excellent new job. But this episode was a turning point in another way. After taking this chance, I was no longer afraid of change. Rather, I became more eager to learn, to grow, and to live up to my potential.

I next worked for Haworth, which is now a privately owned $2 billion office furniture company. While at Haworth, I stayed in touch with the headhunter. I networked her with other friends and colleagues, which gave her the opportunity to develop a specialty—and lucrative niche—in the furniture industry.

Before long, the entrepreneurial urge kicked in for me. First, I went into business with my recruiter friend, but after a year or so I went solo. I developed a specialized, retainer-based search practice for the office and home furnishings industry. That business is now the largest of its kind in the world.

By the time the recession hit in the early nineties, my business was hurting, forcing me to close some offices and let people go. Although it was just me and my cat working out of my house, I always kept up the facade of a larger business while receiving about a thousand résumés a week from unemployed, equally desperate people who I could no longer help. I was interviewing over twenty people a day. Even though I didn't have job referrals at the time, people still wanted to talk. They were desperate for work and for answers about work.

That was the pivotal moment in my own career. I realized I could and should make career and work my main vocation. As a recruiter, I had a unique, insider's perspective on hiring, firing, and the myriad issues that come up every day in the workplace. I got it from both the job-seekers' and the employers' perspectives.

Today, my Web site—www.viscusigroup.com—receives about 100,000 visits each month, and The Viscusi Group is the preeminent retainer-based search practice in the interior furniture industry. When I launched "On the Job with Steve Viscusi" on a small radio station in Westchester, it was an instant hit. We are now a nationally syndicated radio show on almost two hundred markets across North America, and that number is growing every day.

I quickly discovered that people never tire of griping about work and that there was never a shortage of new questions or scenarios to discuss. People were calling in about everyday hassles and predicaments, much more than job-finding and career-planning. Despite all the high-flying long-term advice readily available, no one was talking to people about how to make it through their days on the job. I soon began to appear on other radio shows and national TV, and to be interviewed for various magazines and cited on the Internet.

People endlessly struggle under the weight of deep misperceptions about the realities of the workplace. No one learns in high school or college about when "don't make waves" is the wisest course and when it's better to make yourself visible, for example. Only the fortunate few find mentors to guide them.

I realized that the workforce could use a sort of mentor-in-a-book to explain how work really works—what dynamics and unspoken rules universally govern the worksphere. Once you know the real rules of work and can figure out how to apply them in your own situation, you not only survive work, you thrive in it.

I am not a career counselor or a coach. I have no formal training in the career arena. But I do have expertise as a listener, an entrepreneur, and a radio personality. I am a real person giving real advice based on my real life. This book is a distillation of the down-to-earth lessons I've learned from my parents, from the thousands of candidates I've interviewed, from my many radio show callers, and from running my own business. I've gathered my insights, stories, and advice for optimizing your daily work life and divided them into a simple seven-part framework. Each chapter covers one of the seven primary pieces of our work-life puzzle. By recognizing each piece, you'll be best able to put together a satisfying complete picture.

Chapter 1, Be Here Now: Focus on the Job: In this chapter, I make the singular claim that your career is whatever job you hold today. In other words, wherever you are, this is a perfectly apt place to start applying the ideas and techniques in this book. You don't need to defer anything until later: Be Here Now. You can hold off on the long-range career planning—save it for after-work hours when you can sit down with the classifieds or your Rolodex. Your job now is to learn to do everything the smart way, and to think of your current job as the only one that matters.

Chapter 2, Get Over It: Accepting How Work Works: Work, like life, can be unfair, often infuriating, bizarre, exhausting, and irrational. If you expect otherwise, you're in for a shock. Expectations are the culprit when it comes to disappointment on the job. Chapter 2 shows you how to Get Over It so you can get on with it.

Chapter 3, The Work You: Separation and Boundaries: Once you have the right perspective on job versus career, the next most essential task is to segregate your work persona from the rest of your identity. It's in our best interest to maintain appropriate boundaries between the different spheres of our lives. This can be trickier than it sounds, and requires the development of some specialized skills, which I describe.

Chapter 4, Can You Relate? Workplace Relationships: In all their multiplicity and subtlety, treachery and gratification, relationships are the gears that turn the workplace engine. The substance of work life consists of spending much of the time dealing with other human beings, from managers to subordinates to colleagues. There's a lot to know about making this go smoothly, recognizing hot spots, and coping with problems.

Chapter 5, There's No Such Thing as Small Talk: Communication: Your relationships depend on communication. This section describes insights, tactics, and strategies to allow you to communicate powerfully and comfortably, whether in formal meetings, memos, voice mail, e-mail, or even around the water cooler.

Chapter 6, Juggling on the Job: Organization and Competence: The book up to this point covers emotional territory, which is a huge challenge. But all the people skills in the world won't be enough to keep a job if you fail to come up with "the goods." What are the goods? The highest professional quality of work combined with effective management of your essential resources: time, space, and information.

Chapter 7, Beyond the Job: Career Talk: Although I've back-burnered all the career stuff until now, I owe it to my readers to offer fulfilling ways to go the extra distance: how to coordinate your current workplace life within the larger scheme of career. By concentrating on a few key efforts such as sharing credit, showing grace under pressure, and promoting your ambition in appropriate ways, your day job can lead to the career of your dreams.

Once you've absorbed the cumulative wisdom on these subjects, you'll be well equipped to apply what you've gleaned. My hope is that the book's lessons will get you where you want to be—from nine to five every day for the rest of your working life.

1

Be Here Now:
Focus on the Job

WHAT IS THE DIFFERENCE BETWEEN A career and a job, anyway? A career is the sum of all the jobs you've ever had. A career is described in retrospect. But "work" is what you live every day. Work is what this book is about. It's a supremely important lesson that everyone needs to learn—or to be reminded about from time to time: *Your career is whatever job you hold today. And, further, the way you deal with your current job is what matters most.*

Each step of the way, at every job, you're continually creating your identity, forming habits, and cultivating your values and beliefs. That's why slacking off is so dangerous; not only can it badly damage your reputation, but also, more important, it has a negative impact on your self-esteem. Committing to doing your best and extracting the most value from *where you work now* is the antidote to boredom and burnout.

Although this advice may sound like common sense, oddly enough, there are very few resources available that show how to stay focused on work, at work. Plenty of books offer advice on how to forge a career, assemble a portfolio of skills and connections, and integrate work with outside life—all of which is fine. But these guides usually omit the biggest subject: Most of our work life is spent . . . working.

Your first job is a special case. Any new worker has basics to learn about work life and organizational mores, and it doesn't matter all that much where you acquire them. (This book can shorten the curve by over 50 percent if you pay close attention!)

And don't worry: "Your career is whatever job you hold today" does not mean that you're doomed to remain an executive assistant, that you'll be stuck at a copy shop instead of making it big as a DJ, or that you'll be spending the rest of your life writing ads for kitchen cleansers. What it does mean is that your career is the totality of all your jobs, and each one of them counts. Not equally, to be sure, but you might be surprised by unexpected outcomes of a seemingly lackluster job.

From Niches to Riches

So often, young people become impatient and feel that the job they are doing today is too demeaning to lead to a career. This attitude leads to what I call AADD, or adult attention deficit disorder, the inability to focus on the job at hand. My own work history is a perfect illustration of what can happen if you overcome AADD—a seemingly "menial" job turning out to be the seed of a fabulous career. Let me explain.

My family just happened to live in a house that was located next to a furniture store called The Modern Furniture Barn. I was sixteen when the seventy-two-year-old owner and his wife, Mr. and Mrs. Louis Euster who ran the store day and night, hired me. Our clients were mostly doctors, lawyers, dentists, and other upscale types from throughout the New York metropolitan area and Fairfield County, Connecticut, who were all hungry for the latest craze of bubble lamps and Eames' chairs. I was a file clerk, filing the various furniture catalogs and price lists away during hectic weekends when couples came in to purchase their furniture. I earned $10 an hour, far above the 1979 minimum wage of around $2.75. It was not a typical job for a teenager, but I took it very seriously, distributing catalogs around the store, polishing the various glass tables with Windex, and occasionally going across the street to the local 7 Eleven to pick up Entenmann's and coffee for the staff.

Maybe because my mom had been in retail, I was drawn to selling. So although I wasn't hired to sell, I was always eager to ask or answer a customer's question. Despite the fact that the other salespeople resented my enthusiasm, I found learning about the business both fun and fascinating. I was amazed, for example, at the price of furniture. Could an Eames lounge chair and ottoman for the living room really cost $2,000?

After a year with the company, I received my first promotion: to salesperson for a new discount center in the basement of the store where they sold all the damaged or returned furniture. But I wasn't stuck in the basement for long. Every time someone bought an item from the discount area, they inevitably also wanted to buy a new, good piece of furniture upstairs, so I got to work throughout the store. My wages were raised to about $14 per hour, and within another year, I was selling $5,000 worth of furniture every weekend.

Of course, I hadn't yet absorbed the lessons of this book— I was a normal teenager after all!—and so I was a bit embarrassed by this job. The fact that the store was removed from the town and that local people did not often stop in was a big relief. It meant I didn't have to see my peers every weekend while working.

Meanwhile, I began to develop an affinity for furniture and design and continued to work weekends at the store as I went through college. Just as I was graduating, the company owner asked if I would help him create an office furniture division. It seemed like an exciting offer, the chance to open up almost my own business with someone else's money and have autonomy. Most significant of all at the time was to gain an important-sounding title. My friends were all going to work for IBM, Con Edison, General Electric, and AT&T, and I was going to remain behind at the furniture store—at least now I could say I was a manager.

Two years out of college a recruiter with whom I had been working, trying to hire employees for the furniture store, suggested that I start to go on interviews with Fortune 500 companies in Manhattan. I jumped at the chance and went on my first interview in New York City on Madison Avenue between Sixtieth and Sixty-first streets, the glamour capital of New York City's corporate world. I was more in awe of the real estate than the job, which was not managerial, less money, and in some ways a step backward. My parents were devastated and frightened for me—they both had held the same job forever and were shocked that I would consider such a "radical" move. But the whole idea of being a salesperson with a car and expense account and a glamorous office overlooking Madison Avenue seemed captivating. Between the headhunter's strong-arming and my own intuition, I accepted the position and never looked back.

I thrived in that corporate culture. My exposure to the Fortune 500 environment gave me the tools necessary to open my own head-hunting business in a big-league, big-corporation way.

---

way to go! Joanne is currently chief resident in neurology at a West Coast teaching hospital. Ten years ago she was working her way through college by delivering pizza. Unlikely as it sounds, that job as a "cheese whizzer" (as her friends termed it) provided her with a lot: spending money to sustain her hard-studying existence, as well as several friends she otherwise wouldn't have made, one of whom introduced her to a favorite sport—snowboarding—and another to her fiancé. Joanne treated her pizza gig with respect, and as a result she reaped rewards she otherwise would have missed.

Here's the lesson: This one, narrow niche area—furniture—that I stumbled into while in high school led to a much broader, successful career, including a multimillion-dollar head-hunting business that allowed me to do what I loved to do as a radio and television broadcaster specializing in the workplace. Was it glamorous? No. Was it sometimes embarrassing? Yes. But was it profitable? Was it a real business where I could make real money? Yes, yes, yes!

The Pride Ride

Joanne did not think that as a pre-med she was above that kind of work—delivering pizza—because she's not wired to look at things that way. But pride is a very common trap at the workplace, where some employees believe that certain types of tasks are beneath their dignity. Well, that is total nonsense, and you'll be doing yourself a great favor by giving the boot to any such thoughts or feelings if they ever come knocking. By avoiding the Pride Ride, you gain in a number of ways:

- You seem like a secure person. Only people who question their own dignity worry about losing it.
- You show you're a team player.
- You're aware. When someone ignores one thing— such as the need to pack up all the crates for the upcoming trade show—that person ends up tuning out a lot more—such as the reps at other trade show booths who have market insight to share.
- You're open to opportunity. You don't turn down assignments that might appear beneath you. This doesn't mean that you allow a pattern in which people are consistently handing you mindless work. But don't

be too quick to jump to that conclusion. And if you think such a situation is developing, you don't have to refuse to do the task; maybe mention that you hope your "temporarily helping out" is making a difference.

way to go!   Peter was appalled that his buddy Dave was willing to proofread a quarterly report at the accounting firm where they were both trainees. He told Dave it would set a precedent that would encourage other CPAs to dump their grunt work on him. But Dave didn't mind. He actually enjoyed proofreading, plus he knew Peter was prone to overemphasize what "the others" will think. As he was proofreading, Dave noticed an arithmetical error that would have been deeply embarrassing for the company had it been printed. The upshot: Dave vaulted into notice for being a "will-do" kind of guy, detail-oriented, and the young hero who saved the firm some face.

We all need our share of ego to survive and to thrive. But when we let that part of our personality run the show, it's always bad news for our work lives. A too-insistent ego is always reminding us that wherever we go, its needs come first. I'll go into more detail later in the book, but the following story illustrates the pitfalls of the overactive ego—and one manager's creative, tactical solution.

There is no such thing as a worthless job, and the idea that you will eventually "rise to the occasion . . . down the road . . . when it counts" implies that there are some occasions not worth rising to—and that's bunk. (Plus, you might not even recognize such a "big" occasion unless you've prepared for it by treating the small and medium occasions with respect.) Every job offers unexpected possibilities, opportunities to learn and to enjoy your time, but it's improbable that you'll see these unless you're focused on being where you are. It all comes down to paying attention.

turning tables   Todd ran the Fast Friends delicatessen in Chicago. It was situated close to two acting schools, so a majority of the staff were aspiring actors. After a few years, Todd hit upon a plan to indoctrinate new employees in the realities of restaurant work. In something akin to a college fraternity rush period, Todd gave the newly hired waiters a special T-shirt to wear for their first two weeks on the floor. On the shirts was printed backward: "I Am NOT an Actor. I AM a Waiter." Whenever the fledgling waiter behaved unprofessionally— as virtually everyone did at times during their first shifts, usually by copping an attitude with a client or a kitchen worker or by starting to yak away with a customer—Todd would gently but firmly lead the offender to a big mirror on the kitchen wall. He'd explain, "This T-shirt is telling you more than you may realize. The main thing is that this is where you *work*—and that it's not about *you,* it's about the *work*. The shirt is also explaining everything you need to know to *make really good tips*."

The art and science of workplace dynamics are remarkably similar across the spectrum of job sites. Every job offers a chance to hone your interpersonal perceptions and techniques and to reinforce your better habits while striving to eliminate your weaker ones.

An Equal Opportunity Mantra

Despite its association with Eastern philosophy, there's really nothing alternative or hippie-ish about the phrase "be here now." It's one of the best and wisest pieces of advice going. After all, here is the only place you can be at this moment. The only way to appreciate an experience, make the most of it, and learn from it is by being present and accounted for (to yourself).

The best thing about being here now is that it *frees* you. You're liberated from having to worry about all the coulda-woulda-shouldas of your career up till now, or about what might happen later. You can turn your workday into an experiment, a game, or an adventure. Nothing is preordained. By accepting that your current job is your starting point, you essentially assume responsibility for where you are now and how you handle your day. There's no more need to blame misfortune or bad grades. You now permit yourself to make your work situation as worthwhile as possible.

Freedom is one thing, but without a few ground rules you might end up with nothing left to lose, as the old song goes. Here are some specific freedoms, responsibilities, and suggested coping skills that are part of the package when you really inhabit your current job:

You're free to realize that you can also choose not to be there. You're not trapped and you're not there for someone else's sake. Employees who are unhappy in their jobs nearly always find that once they start actively looking for another position, the day-to-day work becomes infinitely more bearable, all because they know it's finite. (Sometimes an employee even discovers that it's not such a bad fit for him after all, now that he's adjusted his attitude.) Well, you're free to think of it as finite from the get-go, without having to start looking elsewhere.

You're free to keep your sense of humor close at hand—where it belongs! Every workplace is imbued with some absurdity and wackiness. You might as well enjoy it. Sometimes even negative developments can be funny if you don't take them too seriously. When a coworker is trying to jump your place in line for a promotion, it's galling; but once you've neutralized the threat, it's easy to see how petty a spectacle it is—like a Chihuahua chasing after and barking at a vacuum cleaner. As long as you don't go overboard and portray yourself as a goofball, people love having you around, and it makes your own life easier and more fun.

You're free to be smart, do a great job, and feel good about your work. Once you no longer resent being where you are, or strain at the bit to be elsewhere, you owe it to yourself to learn the game as well as possible, and practice it until it becomes second nature. Okay, perhaps you're not yet following your bliss; or maybe you were and your bliss shook you in a crowded train station. Still, successfully grappling with challenges, growing more accomplished, and getting strokes from other professionals are rewarding in themselves.

You're free to make lasting professional connections. Since this job "counts," so do the people you meet—and so do you, to them.

You're free not to bolt prematurely. This is an especially interesting angle. Once you feel some buy-in to your current job, you're likely to weigh company and career jumps more carefully—and wisely. Maybe you would have gotten swept away by the dot.com lure like so many professionals have in the past several years—and many of them go crawling back to the companies they'd hastily abandoned. Or perhaps you'd have realized that such easy money was going to prove a mirage before long, and that jumping from a computer chip company to work for a pet food Web site wasn't such a hot idea anyhow.

You're free to learn and acquire skills. The more knowledge and ability you acquire, the higher you'll rise at your current company, and the more marketable you'll become.

You're free to live well. The whole idea, after all, is to enjoy this existence. If you can think of your work in a positive light, as something that you've actively chosen and that you gain from in a multitude of ways, it becomes a lot easier to leave it behind at the end of the workday. And it sends the strong but subtle message that you're entitled to be comfortable in your professional persona, which means you have the same rights in your private life too. So you can go to the gym, learn to cook, take yoga classes, check out flicks and live music, see your friends often, and salt away some funds so you can take exciting vacations, like white-water rafting or a four-day jazz festival. Finally, you're free to give yourself as much sleep as you need!

In addition to accepting responsibility and embracing freedom, a "be here now" attitude breaks down into the following four ways of approaching your job, which I encourage you to try.

Cultivating Contacts

As the entire recruiting business is centered around who you know—names, contacts—I am a huge believer in networking.

It's one of the few fields where you can actually cash in through friends and people you know. The person recruiting doesn't pay anything—the party hiring does. Those you meet at an "interim" job, however, are just as likely to be valuable contacts and collaborators as those you get to know at longer-term positions.

This point was really brought home to me when I had to find a celebrity to interview for my first major, nationally syndicated show. I racked my brain to come up with someone I knew who would fit the "famous and controversial" requirement. Eventually, I remembered when I was the head of student activities at Manhattan College that, for one program, I had hired Dr. Shere Hite, the author of *The Hite Report on Female Sexuality*.

So I wrote a very humble letter reminding Dr. Hite that not only had she spoken at the college but that I had picked her up in my friend's broken down Dasher on Central Park West. We had gotten a flat tire and the incensed author had stayed outside the car cursing at me for not sending a limo (which we students could not afford). I even sent her a picture I had kept of myself introducing Shere Hite back in 1979. To my amazement I got a call within a week from her publicist who said that she vaguely remembered me and would be delighted to speak with me. If I met with her approval she'd give me an exclusive radio interview. I spoke with her by telephone, and chatted about meeting her twenty years before. By coincidence, one of her favorite skirts ever was the skirt she wore in the picture I'd sent. She seemed to think I would be a gentle interviewer, and agreed to show up at ABC Studios as my very first guest.

Dr. Shere Hite was certainly the first famous-person interviewee of my career. The interview lasted almost an hour and a half. It put my show on the map very quickly—all because I remembered to network and pull that name from way back in college. I'm not 100 percent convinced she really remembered me, but it hardly matters now. Shere Hite has since become a mentor in guiding me through this book and the publishing process. The contact continues!

wrong turn! Tomai proved irresistible from the day she started working at Horizon Consultants, a Philadelphia-based firm that specialized in advising nonprofits. She seemed solid, clever, eager to work and learn, and to genuinely like the people around her. A few of the older workers felt a real closeness with Tomai. Then one day, word whipsawed around the office that Tomai had resigned, and she was going to work for one of Horizon's competitors. Her bearing over the next two weeks revealed that she saw the company as a bump on a log compared to those she had her eyes set on. Several coworkers who'd thought of Tomai as a friend were deeply offended by the abrupt way she flew the coop, and her attitude once she was on her way out. They felt as if she had "played" them. If Tomai ever decides she'd like to reconnect with these people, or to use one as a contact, she'll have her work cut out for her just to return to neutral in their eyes.

The moral is to treat everyone whose path you cross well—you never know when your lives may intersect. Be especially careful to never exhibit a dismissive attitude about an employer by having your sights set elsewhere. It's the kiss of death for earning the trust and respect of coworkers. Long after you leave the workplace you so loudly loathed, you may need those coworker contacts.

Overdelivering

Whatever work you happen to be performing, doing it well makes it more pleasurable, interesting, and gratifying—and earns accolades from bosses and respect from peers.

way to go! Arlene had no plans to go to law school, but she fell into a position as a part-time (thirty hours a week) paralegal after she graduated from art school. It paid her barely enough to cover living expenses, loan payments, and her share of the rent for a studio she shared with three other sculptors. But whatever research or clerical tasks the lawyers assigned her, Arlene would have at them like they were slabs of wax she was modeling. This way, she found, time passed more quickly and she felt as if she were using her brain. Arlene acquired a reputation for precision, thinking on her feet, and an incredibly good attitude. Associates and partners at the firm would save their trickier general research tasks for Arlene. As she really didn't want to take away more than thirty hours a week from her art, the lawyers actually had to negotiate for their turn to give Arlene their work. Despite her status as a "mere" paralegal, Arlene was highly appreciated, and this regard carried over and nourished her as she moved through her other worlds. When one of the associates met an art collector at a conference, he thought of Arlene, and arranged for this collector to see her work, resulting in a three-piece purchase.

way to go! Jeri liked the sales side of the business. Working in the front office of a plastic container manufacturer, Jeri was focused on cutting deals with customers, not haggling with suppliers. She had no interest in what was going on down at the factory-floor level. To ink one of her deals, she had to travel to the client's location, where the company founder *insisted* on taking her around to see the facility. Jeri couldn't really get a handle on all the chemistry of the resin-making process, but much to her surprise she found the actual machinery fascinating. She wanted to know how all the parts fit together, and the client was more than happy to comply. Jeri discovered that every major piece of equipment had its own business story behind it, that the deals that must be made on the purchasing level are just as elaborate as those she looked after, and that the bills of materials and project-management software the plant managers relied on were actually far more complex than the spreadsheets she busied herself with. Starting with the factory tour, Jeri became something of an expert in all the facets of the company's operation. A few years later, Jeri was named executive vice president of sales and operations—a position she was qualified to fill only because she'd developed an interest in the full operation, starting with her visit to the factory.

On-the-Job Schooling

You study whatever you're doing in a number of ways. There's the industry itself, regardless of your intrinsic level of interest. If you work in an MIS (management information system) department, you can learn more about using the company's software than you need to perform the job. It'll challenge your mind a little, which is always invigorating; put you in good stead within the company; and bolster a skill that's marketable elsewhere.

Stay Here Now

The emergence of a new work paradigm over the past couple of decades (owing in large part to rightsizing and all it represents) has led many younger employees to think it's counter-

---

FIVE UNEASY PIECES

These are the messy problems that usually go unaddressed in management literature because they're "not supposed to be" an issue. But reality is reality, and I don't shy away from any topic that has such a huge impact on workplace quality of life.

Money. This one is inescapable: Everyone is obsessed with what they make, particularly as it compares to others. And nearly everyone thinks his or her annual raise is insufficient. Everyone is wealth-mad, and too many employees forget the ultimate rule: Don't discuss money with your coworkers.

Romance and sexual issues. This is a subject with a lot of angles old and new. There are many nuances we'll cover, but most of it boils down to the perennially applicable advice: Be cool. While the business world has changed its position about these matters, discretion is still the only way to go. That

productive or retro to stay too long in any one position or with a particular company—a sign of ambition deficit syndrome. As soon as these workers think they've extracted all the tangible career benefits the position offers, they're out of there. There are indeed situations in which this is the wisest course, but in many cases, the employee has only proceeded through a phase one at the company, and with some ingenuity and perseverance, there are further opportunities just below the

and a clear understanding that this is the activity most likely to explode into serious workplace misery for one or both parties.

Spirituality. Whether it's zealots who insist on kicking off executive meetings with prayer, or millions of professionals seeking deep fulfillment in the workplace, this topic has assumed epic proportions.

Hygiene. Hard to believe, but true: Many workers still don't grasp the requirements of cleanliness, presentability, and avoiding offense. And there's a corollary problem: people who overstep the bounds of propriety in how much personal information they share with coworkers.

Prejudice. Unfortunately, racism, sexism, homophobia, and anti-Semitism are still very much alive. Some people don't get it when they're getting shafted as a result of these disgusting tendencies. And then there are those who see prejudice everywhere—like Woody Allen's character in *Annie Hall*.

surface. You might go farther than you expected, or make a jump that hadn't even occurred to you.

---

a tale of two friends

Frank and Doug graduated from journalism school to-gether, having become friends there. Out of the gate, it looked as if Doug would be the star of the two: He promptly snagged a job at *The Atlantic* and was on his way. Frank, meanwhile, settled into a position with a trade publisher that covered high-tech industries. Doug found the hypercompeti-tive environment at the prestigious magazine was making him miserable, so he bounced elsewhere, to a small literary journal; but then he found that too penny-ante, so he staked out a spot in a trade book house. When he saw that they were starting to publish exclusively gardening and celebrity books, he bolted. Frank, however, stayed put; he sailed up the masthead to become a senior editor, executive editor, and then editor in chief in six years. When he was ready to make his move, he swung into the European senior editor slot for *Time,* a high-powered and high-paying job on the Continent—Frank's dream come true. Doug was still flailing away In a careening career to no place in particular and with little satisfaction along the way. Neither Frank nor Doug really knew exactly what he wanted at the beginning of his career. The difference between them is that Frank had the sense to stick around and acquire skills and responsibilities where it was quite easy to do so, whereas Doug hopped from one half-considered position to another. If he'd been sure in his focus, it would have been a different story. Taking a shotgun approach to your work life doesn't work.

The business world's expectations about employment his-tories has changed drastically over the past decade: The idea of loyalty to a company is a relic of an earlier age (a time before corporations took to firing thousands of people at a clip while increasing CEO compensation by millions of dollars at the same time). Nevertheless, employers still want to see evidence of some consistency and staying power. Anyone who jumps jobs six times in four years doesn't inspire confidence that he'll become a significant contributor to a company.

The Smaller Picture

It is often a commonplace idea that people "can't see the forest for the trees"—they are so caught up in the details that they miss the big picture. But it's just as much of a problem when people miss the trees for the forest, when their perspective is so grandiose that they don't pay attention to the details. In work terms, this means that they fail to learn the ropes *and* enjoy the ride. Too often they're staring into space instead of gleaning every bit of valuable experience from whatever it is they're supposed to be doing. Train your sights on dealing with your current employment situation, not the theoretical future or your master plan. Milk current opportunities before moving on to other pastures.

2

Get Over It:
Accepting How Work Works

BEFORE YOU ENTERED THE REAL WORLD of work, had you imagined it a certain way? Did you envision a nice, cozy, structured situation where all you had to do was show up and do your best to be paid accordingly, enjoy camaraderie with coworkers, receive steady promotions, and go home at the end of the day, satisfied by a job well done?

It's a big shock for most people to discover instead that the working field is not at all level. Things that don't make sense happen all the time. Randomness, chaos, and irrationality yank the rug out from under you over and over. In other words, work, like life, is not fair.

wrong turn!   Brad was thrilled to snag his first job. Although he was only a busboy at an Italian restaurant, he approached it enthusiastically. He trained for three nights without pay, invested in expensive black pants and shoes, and agreed to work whatever last-minute shifts he was needed. He was a quick study and was doing well, learning how to time filling water glasses and juggle large trays of dirty dishes. After his second weekend, he asked for a Sunday off to see his favorite out-of-town baseball team with his dad. They had bought tickets and had been looking forward to this game for months. Brad's manager said, "Sure." So Brad was stunned when he called in that Monday for his week's schedule to be told he was no longer needed. It turned out that Sunday was Mother's Day, the restaurant's busiest day of the year. Apparently, the manager found the mere request for that day off unacceptable. Could he have mentioned this to Brad? Of course! Was it fair? Of course not!

Some work environments are worse than others, of course. But new workers are often most rankled by the elements common to any job. Some of the appalling personal affronts and mistreatment you're expected to endure include:

- ▶ You have to show up *on time, every day.*
- ▶ You have only *one hour* for lunch.
- ▶ You can't *speak* on the phone with friends.
- ▶ You *can't smoke* in the office.
- ▶ You will make mistakes and errors—*and others call them mistakes and errors.*
- ▶ You have only *two weeks of vacation—a year!*
- ▶ You will be *expected* to work late sometimes.

- You *won't* always be appreciated as much as you deserve.
- People will get angry and frustrated with you—*and let you know.*
- People will *not* always say "please" and "thank you."
- People will talk about you *behind your back*.
- Time is *always* of the essence.

This is slightly tongue in cheek. But don't be surprised to find that some of the items really do bother you—a lot. Or to hear little insistent voices inside tell you, "This is unacceptable! No one has to tolerate this kind of thing!"

Then there's the economic dimension. It's virtually inevitable that no matter what you make, it feels like you're being "taken." Here you're busting your butt, working fifty-hour weeks, offering up superb ideas, helping the company attain incredible profits. For your troubles, they pay you as little as possible and bestow piddling annual raises despite stellar performance appraisals. And you're expected to be grateful for receiving a third week of annual vacation time after you've been with the company for five years! Little wonder almost everyone is pretty discouraged by his or her introduction to the real world of work.

The Strategy

So, now that you know the gruesome truth, does it mean you're doomed to a miserable existence while at work? Of course not! That's why you've picked up this book. To stay balanced and get ahead, you first need to accept the fact that your vision of a professional meritocracy, where more accomplished and reliable people steadily rise to the top of the tank, is a sham. You don't want to be miserable all day, muttering to yourself or griping to anyone who'll listen. And you don't want to find you can't leave work behind, because your off time is spent obsessing over some injustice you plan to oppose.

---

wrong turn! Don had negotiated for three months to secure a contract selling his company's newsprint to a large weekly paper in the next state. He'd traveled there on four occasions—the most face-to-face time Don ever had to expend for a medium-size contract. When he made his closing sales call, the purchasing director informed him that the paper's board of directors had instructed him to hold any pending contracts and put them out to bid again from scratch. Don flipped. In front of the rest of his department, Don called the director a few names, cursed the paper, and slammed the phone down. After a closed-door conference with his boss, Don called the director back and apologized. Don kept his job, with a serious warning, but lost both the contract and a lot of respect because he'd blown it so badly. Others would joke around, asking him how the "mad man" was feeling, and he'd have to smile as if it didn't bug him.

While you're practicing acceptance, you also need to find smart, practical strategies for being a satisfied person in a frequently unfair and unpredictable world. You need a coping mechanism so you don't get thrown by any of the inequity, pettiness, immaturity, and abusiveness you might encounter.

You need a point of view that allows you to think clearly and act judiciously, despite all the disappointing and degrading behavior you see in the workplace. Fortunately, there is one very straightforward mental mantra: Get over it!

This phrase is an exceptionally useful attitude to keep in mind. It's like having a built-in coach, someone who wants to see you excel, who knows that a little tough love can sometimes do the trick. The point isn't to break your spirit like a circus pony, but to free yourself to *deal*. If you want to accomplish anything, you can't afford to let reality throw you. Once you get past the emotional noise—self-pity, outrage, irritability, resistance to authority—you're able to create the best opportunities for yourself and to capitalize on every one that comes along.

Get Over It consciousness means a lot more than just buck up! It also means:

Avoid self-pity. Chances are that you have it relatively good if you can take an objective appraisal. In facing the work situation, feeling sorry for yourself will sap your energy and brand you as weak in spirit and drive.

You can handle it. Nearly everyone has faced the same or similar situations, and survived. When you assume you can handle something, you're three-quarters of the way home.

Move forward. The workplace is not as simple as it first appears; there is still a lot more for you to learn—about the company you work for as well as the nature of job dynamics. You need to get past a sense of alienation and establish a provisional comfort level to be fully engaged and get the maximum benefit from a job.

You have options. If you find the modern work world unbearable, America offers other possibilities, such as a rural lifestyle, living and working at travel destinations, telecommuting, job sharing, flex time, planned communities, and so on. Keeping the larger perspective in mind wards off desperation.

Get Over It is as useful in the moment-to-moment as in the day-to-day or year-to-year, because it helps maintain resilience. After all, it's generally not events themselves that trip us up, but rather our reaction to them that can make situations seem unbearable. While other people are not within our control, our responses nearly always are—more so than most of us realize.

---

way to go! When Laura, an accountant at an electronics manufacturer, was laid off on a Friday afternoon, it was a complete surprise. Management had decided to liquidate the accounting department and outsource to a business on the other side of the country. Laura was momentarily shocked, but quickly became incensed. Instead of venting her rage, she decided to take a fifteen-minute walk before packing up her desk. While outside, her anger lifted enough to let some light in. Laura went back to meet with the human resources VP. She remained calm and collected but steely-eyed as she asked for five months' severance pay. Realizing that Laura was understandably infuriated, the VP made a quick assessment and offered her four months. This gave Laura the money she needed to take the time to find a great new position, as well as a few weeks off to visit friends and repaint her garage.

I always advise people faced with similar, potentially explosive situations to take a minimum of a fifteen-minute walk first. Even more preferable is to wait until they've completely cooled off before making a decision or having any adversarial or upsetting conversations. It's so tempting to jump right in and bite someone's head off that I tell people to actually physically leave the office—say they suddenly have a cold, they don't feel well, they have cramps, whatever it takes to go home and cool off. Make the decision overnight and handle it the next day. You'll never be sorry. In fact, such a decompression period often results in a downright positive outcome as the following story illustrates.

Companies Are Not Democracies

Part of why so many people find workplace politics and unfairness so galling is that we're raised to believe that the world is, should be, or someday will be democratic. The will of the majority should prevail, or at least what's best for most should determine policy and outcome. In no way should you perceive the workplace as a democracy or as a democracy-in-the-making. Save yourself some angst and accept this now: *Companies are dictatorships.* (The one exception might be the employee-owned company, but even there, whoever owns the bigger stake will ultimately have the louder voice.)

Some dictatorships are more benevolent than others. Some are more responsive to popular sentiment. But all have a common element: What the dictator says, goes. The company dictator might be the pleasant CEO you pass in the hallway,

DON'T TAKE IT THE WRONG WAY

Get Over It is simple but very strong medicine, so be sure you take it only the way it's prescribed. Get Over It does *not* mean any of the following:

▶ *Just give up.* Get Over It means accept that this is what the situation is now. Some things will forever stay that way—for example, supervisors will *never* appreciate it if you go over their heads with a complaint. But other conditions change all the time—for example, you work for the most incompetent manager in the firm, but she just got a job offer from another (unsuspecting) company. Situations that seem immutable today may be more fluid next year. Conversely, an opportunity that was ripe last month might be all dried up by now.

▶ *Don't care so much.* Get Over It means changing what you can, accepting what you can't, and having the wisdom to know the difference. Crusaders for change need to get over it or they'd be too blocked with rage to function. It doesn't mean not to try to make a difference.

▶ *Forgive and forget.* There's no reason you should pretend nothing ever happened when another worker has been bad-mouthing you to the boss. Get Over It means defuse the emotional charge so you can clearly understand what really happened, prevent any recurrences, and, if it's called for, figure out a workable strategy for appropriate, professional retribution.

or it might be the board of directors in Zurich. No matter, your rights are very limited. Acknowledging and accepting the dictatorship stanches the futile energy flow caused by a preoccupation with fairness.

If you want to be a crusader for social and economic change, fine. If you think it's disgusting that on average CEOs are making thousands of times more than the lowest-bracket workers, there are others who agree. But be clear about this: Going to work and dealing with your job every day is an entirely separate issue. You need to decide whether you can work for any given company, whether you can abide what they do in the world and how they treat their people. That is your decision to make. But you should assume that the company does not care very much what you decide. When you work for a company, what the company cares about is this and only this:

- ▶ You do what you are told to do, in a timely manner.
- ▶ You do it well.
- ▶ You do not cause more trouble than you are worth.

This might sound harsh. Indeed, it is harsh. But when push comes to shove, that's what it boils down to. Obviously, a small, socially responsible firm like Tom's of Maine has a different attitude toward its workers than, say, ExxonMobil does. At some companies, you'll find true compassion on all levels. The point is to not trip yourself up on thinking that things "should be different" than they are; doing so will only introduce an entire world of expectations. Do your job with the assumption that mercy is not part of the equation. This way you'll never get in the habit of relying on mercy.

All of which is to say, once again: Get Over It.

Avoid the Expectation Trap

Expectations—a merger between a sense of entitlement and the belief that life indeed is a *little* fair—are the principal offenders underlying numerous workplace conflicts and personal dissatisfaction. The fewer you have, the better.

Entitlement is an illusion. Sure, you're entitled to be treated in a humane fashion, but if you're not, then . . . you're entitled to quit (unless you think the infraction warrants a lawsuit, which, generally speaking, is an atrocious idea). And no, life is not even a little fair.

---

way to go! Joel, a college student interested in economics, was set on finding an internship with a Wall Street firm. When that proved impossible, he reluctantly took a part-time job with a public opinion polling firm to do computer data entry. He assumed it would be deadly boring and no more than a way to earn a few bucks. Contrary to his expectations, the work wasn't as bad as he thought. He quickly adjusted his thinking and threw himself into doing an efficient job. Within a week, his talent was recognized and he was assigned to a significant new electronic commerce project that he finds fascinating. On top of that, he received his first raise.

The worst aspect of expectations is that they choke off other possibilities and blind you to outcomes that might be even more favorable than what you were anticipating.

Holding on to expectations is not the same as having a plan or goals. A good plan includes alternative scenarios: If plan A doesn't work, I'll try plan B. Expectations tend to be more rigid, focused on one outcome only. They create a state of emotional entitlement: All I have to do is sit back passively and expect to get something. Goals are what you keep striving for proactively without necessarily getting discouraged. Expectations are the deal you make with yourself or other people, and when "the other side" doesn't come through as you wanted, you're left disappointed and off balance.

Entitlement-based expectations can pollute a person's work ethic badly enough to destroy careers.

way to go! Jen came from a wealthy family in northern New Jersey, had attended Cornell, and was gorgeous to boot. When she landed a highly coveted though low-paying job at the New York public TV station, she expected to be an assistant producer within a year and a full producer within three. She didn't endear herself to many people at the station, however, and she acquired a reputation for being unwilling to do the mundane dirty work that constitutes half of everyone's responsibilities, not to mention being an obvious flirt around the executives. About fifteen months after Jen's arrival, an associate producer promotion was announced. Jen went ballistic when she heard that the tap had gone to Hillary, who'd been there less than a year but had been doing a fantastic job, pitching in everywhere she could, and coming up with brilliant programming ideas every week. When Jen stormed into the station manager's office and threatened to quit, he told her, "Well, Jen, no one here would dream of holding you back from pursuing other opportunities." Jen impetuously carried through with her threat and wound up at a much less prestigious local cable station.

Jen's story reminds me of a policy I've tried to follow. I first learned it from General Electric CEO Jack Welch, who says he generally won't hire Ivy Leaguers for top executive spots, because he has found that non-Ivy people have more to prove—and work harder.

From the Unreal to the Real

At the very least, limit yourself to realistic expectations. How do you find out what's realistic? By seeking information from coworkers, consulting other people in the industry, and looking through trade magazines, Web sites, and books. The annual salary surveys in trade magazines, for example, can be great guideposts to channel your sense of what you're worth.

When it comes to your supervisor, it's perfectly legitimate to ask any of the following (although not at one time!):

▶ How long should I expect it to take to make it to the next rung up the ladder?

▶ What responsibilities could I start to take on that will help you out?

▶ How long do people spend in the industry before they run a department? Get an executive position?

▶ Are there any especially interesting, rewarding, or challenging projects coming up in which I could participate? If I don't have the required skills or experience yet, what do I have to do to bridge that shortfall?

There's a subtle but important distinction between showing initiative by asking such questions and becoming a pest,

ANATOMY OF A HIGH-MAINTENANCE EMPLOYEE (HME)

The central requirement in learning how to comport yourself at work is this: Don't be a pain in your boss's neck. Because the last thing you want is for your boss to go home and refer to you as an HME. HMEs are the first to be fired in times of trouble regardless of how good they are at their jobs. When promotions are considered, bosses look for low-maintenance employees—those who are easy to manage, comfortable to work with, and don't need constant pats on the back. Formal qualifications often fall by the wayside; in fact, a highly qualified HME can be the biggest scourge of all to a manager.

HMEs are characterized by some combination of the following traits. If any of these describe you, it's time to make some adjustments.

Ask too many questions. There's a subtle but important distinction between showing initiative by asking questions and becoming a pest. HMEs are incorrigible questioners, and the questions tend to be annoying or irritating, demands for too much information too quickly and too specifically. For instance: "When will I get my next raise?" "Which projects will be cut if the department budget is scaled back? Are any of mine on the line?"

Require micromanagement. HMEs are so concerned about making mistakes or being blamed for something that they're incapable of showing initiative, applying creativity, or working things out with other employees on their own. The manager is constantly drawn in to every deliberation, asked for guidance on every step, no matter how trivial. Delegating to an HME increases a manager's workload, rather than decreases it.

Create interpersonal squabbles. HMEs often have stunted social development. They don't know how to play the political games, communicate with dexterity, shrug off minor insults, be tactful in sensitive situations. They're liabilities for maintaining collegiality on the job, and in fact are frequently the source of feuds.

Complain and whine. HMEs get on a manager's nerves not merely by griping in general but also by yammering about situations that can't be changed and that everyone else has learned to live with—slow elevators, a faulty voice mail system, too much air-conditioning, not enough heat. The size of their office is also a common complaint.

Expect exceptions to be made. HMEs often have an overactive sense of entitlement and demand that their supervisors make special accommodations, bend the rules, or ignore transgressions. They go beyond the "squeaky wheel gets the grease" threshold.

or what I call a high-maintenance employee (HME). High-maintenance employees want to know too much information too quickly, too specifically. For instance: When will I get my next raise? What day? The most important thing is not to become an HME. You never want your boss going home and telling his wife or her husband that "Jimmy is a high-maintenance employee." In times of trouble and when promotions are considered, beyond any qualification, the one thing I think a boss thinks about most is looking for low-maintenance employees—employees who are easy to manage and comfortable to work with.

When Bad Things Happen to People Who Ask for It

You may have seen the bumper sticker "No one can hurt your feelings without your consent." Well, there's quite a bit of truth in the adage. Most of the time, employees who are trampled or shunted aside, whether by commission or omission, were asking for it. People who seem to tumble from one calamity to the next obviously have adopted dysfunctional patterns. But even subtle behavior can eventually undermine your job security.

Every office has a whipping boy or girl. I'll never forget my friend Wayne, an above-average real estate company department head who did a better-than-average job. Wayne was also extremely introverted and nearly perverse in his reluctance to communicate with other staff members. He had this stubborn idea that he did his job and did it well and therefore personal communication was not necessary. *Wrong.* Every time there was a corporate problem or mistake, Wayne's boss seemed to take the brunt of the problem out on him. No matter what— the contract was lost, a file was missing—Wayne was to blame.

To my amazement he absolutely refused to confront his peers or superiors with the fact that he had nothing to do with whatever the problem was. Knowing he would never deny his guilt resulted in his coworkers continuously blaming Wayne for everything. It was simply too easy.

Wayne allowed himself to become the department's ritual sacrifice and continued to be throughout his career. I often reminded him that nice guys finish last, that information was power, and that it was essential that he make people aware that he was "on" to what they were doing to him. He continued to feel that he didn't need to dignify what they were doing, and considered it beneath him to stoop to their level. What did he achieve? Nothing! He continued to trudge through his career; he is now, in his late forties, at the same level he's always been: a downtrodden mid-manager.

How to Know If You're Asking for It

The following questions describe common danger points and behaviors that put an employee at risk for being victimized. Be as honest with yourself as possible. It might be an unsettling exercise to potentially expose your insecurities. But it's a small risk with a big payoff if it helps you pull the wool off even one blind spot.

Do you find yourself left out of key communication loops? Knowledge is power, so cluelessness is weakness. If you're always the last to know about something happening in the office, whether it's an interpersonal hassle or a professional development, then you need to cultivate better information channels.

Instead of waiting for the situation to change, take proactive steps to request publications, memos, reports, and such.

Do you let it pass when someone insults you? Those perceived to be softies become easy targets for peers and supervisors. If someone makes a comment that oversteps your boundaries, particularly if they do so in front of others, call them on it immediately; ask what they meant. Don't appear ruffled; be firm.

Are favors a one-way street? If you give a quid, it's reasonable to expect a quo in return, not immediately but at some point. If you see that another employee is happy to borrow from you but never to lend, turn down further requests for help. People usually know when they're taking advantage of someone, and they know that when someone changes the rules it's because they've had enough.

Do you hold yourself aloof from your coworkers? You don't have to be a good-time Charlie, but a standoffish odd-man-out is an easy target when snafus crop up. If the group goes out for drinks every other Friday, join them from time to time.

Do you take sides? It's a carryover from schoolyard days: When someone you like is having a tiff with another worker or group of workers, you may become hostile to the other party yourself, a version of "the enemy of my friend is my enemy." This is a very unwise and childish pose to assume. Your friend might be wrong in this situation; plus, the antagonist hasn't done anything offensive to you.

Are you too ready to raise your hand and accept blame for errors or problems? This is tricky—sometimes it's a good thing, a sign of professionalism, integrity, and confidence to own up to a problem. Other times, though, you're just offering to take the fall for those who share responsibility.

Be Prepared

Many professional boats have sunk because the captain was blindsided. Some people believe their virtues—i.e., hard work, upbeat attitude, fair treatment of others—will protect them from attack. If it were only so straightforward!

People aren't always who they seem—plus, many people are emotionally volatile, and therefore inconsistent. Always bear in mind the possibility that someone will try to take advantage of you, do you ugly, or snipe. Some people are so smooth that you're not even sure whether they've played you. If you're a naturally trusting sort, then befriend someone who isn't and learn the ropes from him or her. You probably wouldn't want to go through life as a compulsive paranoid, but to some extent the price of your peace of mind and work life is eternal vigilance. Don't let your guard down. Or, to use a more easygoing axiom, follow the Boy Scouts' advice: Be prepared.

One good way to help ensure you won't be suckered is by getting into the habit of asking yourself proactive questions such as:

- ▶ Why do my coworkers want to know that information?
- ▶ Was my supervisor telling me the truth?
- ▶ Is that project in my best interest, or is it a quicksand pit that'll make me appear inept?
- ▶ Should I put that conversation in writing by sending a follow-up memo?
- ▶ Why is she suddenly sharing unsolicited gossip with me?

way to go!   A regular caller to the show, Dennis, was a mid-level employee in an enormous Fortune 500 company. One day he was going to the controller's office to be reimbursed for some business trip expenses. While on line with his expense forms, he heard the secretary behind the counter tell the controller, "I just got a call from the marketing department. That guy Dennis is coming down to get reimbursed and they asked us to do it right away." The controller asked, "Who's Dennis?" to which the secretary replied, "That artsy/fartsy guy." The employees were talking low among themselves, but their implication that Dennis was gay or a little fey was clear. Dennis heard the entire conversation. When his turn came, he asked for the controller, saying, "Tell Mr. Connor the artsy/fartsy guy from marketing is here." The secretary was stunned and turned red. Mr. Connor was practically speechless. He looked at Dennis and said, "Oh, my God, I didn't know you were standing there. I'm so sorry, I sincerely apologize." This six-figure-income-earner was terribly embarrassed in front of the well-dressed thirty-two-year-old marketing assistant. Dennis knew that between today's laws and standards and corporate philosophies that he had Mr. Connor's job in his pocket. Was it worth filing a complaint about? No. It was better to make a friend out of one of the most powerful executives in the company. So Dennis stayed silent about what had happened, although he had made his point clear. From then on, he received nothing but the utmost respect from the controller's office and attributed a later promotion to a recommendation from Mr. Connor, who became a close friend and ally.

This type of inquiry will help you think defensively, spot any weak points in a situation, a plan, or even an argument. One of the first pieces of advice given to student drivers is to drive defensively. If you see what *could* come down, then you'll be ready with a Plan B . . . and C. Not only will this save you from ambushes, but it'll help you optimize everything else you do at work.

Basically, information—knowledge—is power. Never hold yourself aloof from your peers. Don't participate in gossip, but stay within the gossip circle to know what everyone is saying about each other and, more important, what is being said about you. Don't be afraid to speak up, in the most polite way, about things you've heard someone say. They will know in the future that they cannot create a rumor or a lie about you because you will confront them—as opposed to most people, who are afraid of confrontation. People are always embarrassed when they are caught talking or gossiping, and you will immediately put the person on the defensive in a positive way.

Stay Out of the Line of Fire

Employees who keep a low profile tend to avoid land mines or shrapnel, but they also fail to win decorations. Jumping into difficult situations to save the day is a great move if you pull it off. If you blow it, though, you end up in worse shape, status-wise, than if you'd simply sat it out. So beware of heroics.

You have to strike a balance by knowing the difference between safe and danger zones. Safe situations are those where tension hasn't reached meltdown levels—and where you're sure you know what you're doing. Dangerous situations are crises where people are behaving in a volatile fashion or you're not sure of your footing. Don't volunteer to take on a sophisti-

BACK TO THE NURSERY

After the idealism and good times of college, on-the-job reality offends your sense of fairness and entitlement. You see some people ignore, bend, or break workplace rules whenever it suits them. You're astounded to see grown people demonstrate such colossal immaturity and vindictiveness. Here are a few examples of behavior that wreaks havoc:

Deceit. The most talented graphic designer at the firm is completely eclipsed by her self-promoting department manager, who takes credit for his staffers' output.

Abuse. One of the marketing vice presidents has it in for your supervisor, haranguing him all the time about his lousy sales performance—although it's identical to that of the other department managers, who don't get hassled at all.

Favoritism. Your officemate is the department's teacher's pet, and she milks her can't-do-wrong status by talking on the phone to her

cated desktop publishing project on a crash deadline when all you know is basic word processing.

Sometimes you might think it's worth giving it a shot, even without a net, because the potential payback is so high. But that's a risky move, and not generally advisable. If in doubt, sit it out.

boyfriend for hours each day, but when your supervisor sees you conversing with a coworker for a few minutes, he asks to have a word with you in his office.

Backstabbing. Whenever one of the editorial assistants is late for work, the other assistant always manages to rat him out by directing their mutual editor to ask the missing party a question.

Jealousy. One coworker is obsessed with the relative size of her office; another bristles when any of his department peers is praised in the Monday morning staff meetings.

Competition. When the product development division was broken up into teams, the level of pitched opposition among them was scary; worse than that, though, was the savage clawing for status within each team.

Gossip. You're boggled by the degree of cliquishness you encounter. Some days it seems as if all the conversations are hushed, and you wonder when any actual work gets accomplished.

Unfairness and Setbacks

The truest test of an employee's mettle is how he or she handles a crisis among personnel. The crisis might be getting passed by for a coveted promotion or juicy project. (Here's where expectations can really slice you to ribbons.) Perhaps it's a concerted campaign to oust a certain worker. Or a project coordinator is trying to fob off blame for a lame result on one of the consulting engineers. There are limitless possibilities in the workplace for backstabbing, blame-shifting, character assassinating, and so on.

Whether the aggrieved party is innocent or really has messed up isn't as important as the way that person comports him- or herself. Grace under fire is universally admired, whereas wobbling under pressure is seen as weakness. A low-worth player can emerge from a firestorm with much upgraded status. A well-liked, competent manager can wind up smeared and defeated.

If you have a reliable mentor in your life, the time to consult with him or her is during a workplace crisis. Meanwhile, the following describes how much is really on the line—and what a huge impact your response to workplace problems will have on the overall situation:

Outcome of the situation at hand. If you stay cool, carefully marshal your resources (i.e., allies), maintain professionalism, and move swiftly and intelligently to take countermeasures, the likelihood that you'll prevail is high. But if you freak out, gripe, rant, demand help from coworkers, or act out unprofessionally, you're shooting yourself in the foot. It's better to have someone owe you.

Likelihood of follow-up hassles. There's a dynamic on the job called "mobbing," which means in essence that people revert to behaviors associated with lower rungs of the evolutionary (or career) ladder. Someone who's on the ropes will continue to get pummeled, become the sacrificial victim, just like the poor kid who was mercilessly bullied in the schoolyard (the geek who's now worth a cool $250 million in Silicon Valley). A worker who's lost a major battle often gets pushed out of the company within a couple of years. Likewise, someone who's nobly weathered a tough fight is unassailed again for a long while; it's an unspoken tenet of fair play.

Net effect on the worker's reputation at the company or in the industry. Everyone will remember how you handled the situation. It will be seen as a defining episode. Your behavior will be deemed a microcosm of your overall character.

Impact on the employee's self-regard. This is immeasurably important—it's the most important intangible of all. Even someone who's reputation has been smeared in a cesspool can still pick up and move on—in career, in life—as long as his or her self-esteem wasn't irreparably damaged.

Maintaining workplace relationships. If you pulled your friends into your conflict without their express agreement, they're unlikely to have much trust or respect left for you. And if you harangued them with every knock-down-drag-out detail throughout the ordeal, they probably will want a good long vacation from you. But if you maintained humor, interest in their lives, dignity, professional standards, and a sense of propriety while being raked over the coals, then your friends will not only love you the more for it, they'll regard you with a bit of awe.

How to Run a Reality Check

If you think someone is out to get you at work, but you're not quite sure, you can take several tacks to find out. One way is to ask one or several people you trust whether they've heard

WHAT A SHAME

Some people never learn how to Get Over It. Make sure you don't become one of these archetypes:

▶ *The Reformer.* Someone who's jousting at windmills rarely realizes it till long after the fact. Not only was he wasting valuable time and energy by trying to take on the system, but he was making a fool of himself in the process. People give him a wide berth.

▶ *The Dreamer.* Someone who's always wishing things could be different will recommend unrealistic solutions, say too much in some situations, or intrude where she's not wanted. Idealism goes a lot farther and does more good outside the workplace than within. No one takes her seriously.

▶ *The Cynic.* Embittered by the foul realities of the work world, the cynic has a snide word to say about every situation. His irreverence lets everyone know that he's chosen to be an outsider. He never gets a promotion or goes anywhere.

▶ *The Crab.* The situation is so vexing that she ends up taking her anger out on nearly everyone around her—such as all those coworkers who are in the same boat as she. Everyone tries to avoid her, or else they treat her like a dangerous chemical.

▶ *The Oddball.* This is the guy who wears mismatched socks, drinks boiled water instead of coffee or tea, and plays with plastic soldiers on his desk. He just wasn't made for the work world—he's made sure of that.

anything is amiss. But doing that exposes you to the risk of your concern getting back to the other party.

In most cases, the best approach is to confront the person directly, one to one. Simply ask if there's any problem, because you thought you noticed some tension in the air between the two of you. This might prompt an honest, open discussion that will clear the air. Or the could-be protagonist may deny there's a problem, say it must be in your head. In which case, you could say you're reassured, because while of course you assumed that he'd address any problem directly, the vibe had seemed a little strange.

You've let him know that *you know* something is up, and cut into his maneuvering room: If he has any conscience, he'll be aware of how much of a liar he is whenever he disses you after this encounter. You have the high moral ground, which is actually quite a tangible asset in office politics.

Great Opportunities vs. Danger Zones

The following examples illustrate the difference between situations where it's smart to get involved and those to be avoided. Remember, when you go for any of these types of good opportunities, you must be standing on solid ground—don't go too far beyond your knowledge and competence zones.

Great Opportunities

1. The marketing department is looking for someone in your department to help familiarize new sales staff with your company's line of goods.

Advantage: This is a very strategic and high-profile assignment. It involves you with the money-making side of the business. And it's a great opportunity to forge important connections.

2. An employee falls ill and the company needs someone in a pinch to attend the big annual convention in Chicago.

Advantage: This is a wonderful opportunity to establish contacts throughout the industry and gather large-spectrum learning about your field. Plus, you're likely to participate in the debriefing process after the show, expected to offer your insights and report back to top managers.

3. Your boss wants someone to help her make a presentation at the office of a key client.

Advantage: Likely to be an excellent chance to bond with your supervisor and establish a "face" presence with the customer.

4. Your firm has just implemented a companywide enterprise resource management (ERP) software program, and wants one person in each department to become the resident expert.

Advantage: Potentially, this will make you indispensable; the knowledge will dramatically raise your marketability quotient, and even open up entirely new career avenues; you have opportunity to interface with every department in the company. *Caveat:* This could be extremely time-consuming and headache-fraught. Make sure beforehand that the software installation has been going smoothly, and that compatibility problems aren't rampant.

5. Company profits are steady, but management wants another Big Hit to drive growth. They've started to assemble a

new product design team, incorporating a mix of people from production and marketing, to design and test-market a new line.

Advantage: This is a highly strategic project that will get a lot of attention from company honchos. Much of what you'll learn about new product development will be very entrepreneurial, which is always valuable. The pace of work will likely be brisk, and everyone will be highly enthusiastic. Even if the specific product development flops, the experience itself, contacts, and marketable skill-building will make it thoroughly worthwhile for you. Plus, when new teams are organized, your name will automatically be in the running. *Caveat:* Whenever top management is involved directly in a project, the problems they cause, and when they cause them, tend to be on a scale to match their self-importance; be ready to hunker down and bite your tongue if and when seriously silly decisions are taken.

Danger Zones

1. Your supervisor needs someone in the department to conduct a wide-ranging market research survey, and says it will help save the company money by doing it in house.

Disadvantage: You'll generally be expected to carry out a project such as this in addition to your normal workload, and this will mean a vast amount of overtime. Many research surveys are tedious, unexciting work, and so the amount you'll actually learn from doing the project won't be enough to compensate—you'd gain nearly as much from reading the final report. It's not the type of project guaranteed to high-profile your name or pull much appreciation. And any company that looks to save money this way is taking advantage of its people.

2. Your supervisor is keenly competitive with another

department manager. She asks if you'd care to work on a project in which there'll be some interdepartmental collaboration.

Disadvantage: The pitfall here is that you'll be tarred by the brush of the feud—you're the envoy sent to the enemy

IN YOUR DREAMS

The word *expect* has a number of connotations. (It's pregnant with meaning!) Some expectations are fair and reasonable, reality-based, while others are so wildly out of line with real life that they're destructive fantasies. While I urge you to avoid the disappointment inherent in dreamy built-in entitlements, it's perfectly within your rights to expect certain things in work life. If you work for an employer, you expect to be paid. If you treat a coworker with decency, you expect the same in return.

The following scenarios include real-life and fantasy expectations. In which category do you recognize yourself?

SITUATION: On short notice, you prepared an excellent sales report that your boss presented to his supervisor, the divisional VP.

In your dreams: Your boss will cite you to the VP as the writer of the report. (You can require, of course, that your boss tell the truth if the VP asks him who wrote it, but you're not likely to be privy to that moment.)

Real life: Your boss acknowledges to you his

camp. Everyone will associate you with the wasteful contest your manager creates at work. It's not a good way to get in your manager's good graces, because she's not being good or gracious.

appreciation for your fine and timely work. You can ask to have the acknowledgment in writing, to add to your ongoing work references.

SITUATION: You were the originator of the concept for a new magazine at the publishing company where you work, and it is launched.

In your dreams: You are appointed as the magazine's editor, receive a large bonus or raise, and a promotion. (At many companies, all or most of this would happen, but you can't demand it.)

Real life: Public acknowledgment of your specific role.

SITUATION: You stay late at the office—until 9:30 P.M.—for nine days running to help finish a massive industrial-site design project. As per the employee manual, the company provided dinner and cab fare each evening.

In your dreams: A free day off. (In most companies, this would be out of the question, though perhaps very few managers would raise an accusatory eyebrow if you took a single sick day just after the project was polished off.)

Real life: Acknowledgment and appreciation.

3. Someone needs to go to Pennsylvania to supervise a big printing job—they need a company person there to sign off on each of the runs.

Disadvantage: This is dull, thankless stuff, and you're unlikely to make any valuable contacts. It takes you away from home base, where your work will pile up, and if any problems crop up, you might miss even more desk time than you expected to.

4. A new product launch has gone desperately amiss, hemorrhaging money for the past several months and falling shy of the department's quality projections. They need an assistant supervisor to help grab it by the horns.

Disadvantage: This is a high-risk, high-tension situation with a good likelihood of failure. Even if you and the team get the situation under control, it's already cost the company a bundle, so you won't create new gain so much as prevent further damage, which is relatively thankless.

5. The company is relocating to another building in a different neighborhood, and each department needs to select a point person to work with human resources and building logistics in both locations to ensure that everything arrives where it should, intact.

Disadvantage: This is an enormous hassle that will take you away from your real work and place you in a situation where everyone is demanding to know where his or her coffee mug went.

3

The Work You: Separation and Boundaries

YOUR WORK PERSONA IS NOT IDENTICAL with your nonwork-life personality. People who think they must always try to be true to their real selves on the job tend to be frustrated, bitter . . . and naive. It's a major misconception to think that there is only one true way for you to be and to go about living, and that anything that deviates from this represents a loss of integrity. When you go to work, it entails a special way of being you—what I call the Work You. The bottom line is that there's not merely one You, but many: the Friend You, the Family You, the

Boyfriend You, and so on. And it's imperative that you get your Yous straight.

A solid Work You will diverge at times from your notions about the Real You. The circumstances alone make this clear; after all, would the Real You choose to situate itself in a honeycombed matrix of workstations and work surfaces (as opposed to desks)? This environment tells you, in explicit terms, things are different here. And this means that your job determines your behavior, not the other way around.

In general, the workplace is not a forum for self-expression, and anyone who thinks otherwise is laying the groundwork for self-sabotage. While "follow your bliss" is a great sound bite, when it comes to making it through the work routine, the adage doesn't make much sense. Nobody can steer their way through traffic by consulting the stars. For daily navigation, you need a down-to-earth guidance system, one that will impose some restrictions that don't seem to have anything to do with bliss. Above all, you need to figure out what you can bring to work and what you should leave at home.

We all have many aspects to our personalities. The fact that we sometimes have to suppress some of these should not be seen as an imposition or a stifling of creativity. Rather, it's merely adjusting to the implicit boundaries that allow us to cooperate. There's a worthwhile trade-off here: In exchange for adapting your behavior slightly to a work context, you get to earn a living and, hopefully, derive gratification from the challenges and opportunities inherent in your job.

Whenever I interview someone who doesn't seem to get the Work You concept, I always find that the person is suffering from misconceptions or delusions. Some of them fail to

way to go! Bob was a "smartest guy you've ever met" type with a difference: He liked to air his working-class Brooklyn accent and the peppery choice of language that accompanied it—partly because his combination of brilliance and vulgarity forced people to take a look at their prejudices. Speaking with a broad accent and employing an unending stream of four-letter action words, Bob was a most unusual CPA. At his firm, however, Bob was the go-to guy when any especially complicated problems popped up. He had the knack of looking at balance and profit/loss spreadsheets as if they were musical scores and pinpointing the underlying patterns. He could tell right away if a client was cooking the books (no matter how expertly) or if a company's in-house bookkeeper had neglected a tax code angle. But after four stellar years, the firm still hadn't made him a partner, though he was partner material. Bob asked the managing partner what was up, and found out that his down-and-dirty tone had rubbed a couple of key clients the wrong way, which, yes, had influenced the firm's decision. He agreed to cool it, when meeting with clients and at the office, and within the month Bob was made a partner. Bob would always have an earthy quality, of course, but keeping its expression within accepted parameters at work was the mature approach. He found that the change felt very positive—as if he were shedding part of a burden he'd been carrying from adolescence.

realize that this isn't a dress rehearsal—your current job is *not* like a community college before you move on to the real world of a university. And sometimes they refuse to accept that the world is the way it is. But most of the time, these burgeoning professionals are clinging to an erroneous view of how seamless work and life should be, like they can walk off one set and onto the other without changing anything. I try to instill a more realistic understanding about work, but sometimes it takes me a few tries before a light flicks on.

Guidelines for a New and Improved Work You

There's no way to define a single best Work You personality. Fortunately, we're too diverse for a single template to apply across the board. If you're a very verbal person, for example, you're going to deal with situations differently from someone who's more purely analytical and numbers-oriented. Some people are more naturally inclined to influence others around them, and they might make superb managers (or dangerous cult leaders). I can't advise every worker in the world as to what personality he or she should have. But there are a number of primary principles to help you find the right fit between the Work You and the rest of your personality.

Creating a Work You is a process, involving some trial and error, but the more you can figure out off the job, the better. Without getting obsessive over it, use your off time to figure out how you want to appear and behave, so that you can hit the ground running when the work week comes around. Learning on the job is one thing, but figuring out who you are on the job is another. That's why the following ideas are intended for you to mull over, rather than apply on a moment-to-moment basis. These are intended to help you develop some strategic awareness. Once you do, the tactics follow naturally.

Downplay your prickly parts. For many people, the whole point of a Work You is to exercise some restraint; too much personality is dangerous on the job, especially if that personality has a serious edge. If you consider yourself an irreverent, iconoclastic sort, for example, that doesn't mean it's smart to exercise your scathing wit at work. Enjoy your barbed thinking, write a column for a paper, make your friends' guts ache from laughter. But if you go around planting zingers on the job, some of the honchos will consider you a loose cannon. Any small thrills you derive from your antics will be thoroughly overshadowed by your loss of professional prestige. In most work environments, you can't be a rebel without a cost.

Inevitably, some people are more politically formidable in the workplace, while others are more lackadaisical. What I tell the aggressive ones—the bullies, backbiters, snipers, maulers, and abusers—is to be careful not to eat themselves alive with their own drive, and to warn them off from making life horrible for others—the what-goes-around-comes-around notion. Because when these types take a fall, there are a lot of people who delight in watching them go down in a fireball. As for the more laid-back workers, I advise them to cover their backs and at least recognize when things are conspiring against them.

Avoid impulsiveness. The Work You puts a premium on deliberate action. At work, you never want to shoot from the hip, or allow emotions to throw you off your game. Whenever callers tell me they lost it with someone, they always say they regretted it afterward because it made them look weak or foolish. You don't want to show that you're thin-skinned, shaky, or vindictive. Another reason to hold your fire is that just about everyone regrets it when they blurt something out—especially if it's a hurtful comment or opinion.

Be strong. At work, you should take care that your words and actions don't reveal too much about your private life. You should especially avoid revealing any personal weaknesses or painful events. This way, you deny potential enemies ammunition, and you also eliminate any need for pity or conciliation. Anyone who has to be treated with kid gloves is hard to take seriously. No matter how fragile you might feel at times, always present a sturdy visage at the workplace.

Keep 'em guessing. It's never good to be typecast. When the other workers have you pigeonholed as the soccer mom or the Knicks fan, you've been reduced from a person to a tag. Anyone who's become a known quantity or an open book has no mystique left, and interesting possibilities don't present themselves very often to workers whose flair has fizzled.

It's far better to keep 'em guessing—surprise your co-workers periodically so you don't get typecast. Don't be 100 percent predictable, for example, in your dress style. Every now and then, wear something a little more elegant. Even if you don't actually have a romantic date after work that day, let others wonder if you do—plus, you'll send the message to yourself that you can. Don't be flighty and eccentric just for kicks, but work some change-up pitches into your style. Being unpredictable doesn't mean you're unreliable but that you're *interesting.* If you're highly opinionated about everything, your peers tend to discount some of those judgments, but if you're *selectively* opinionated, then your assessments have more meaning.

Have a life! Here's the big secret: The key to fashioning a Work You is to make sure your Nonwork You is alive and kicking. It may seem a little paradoxical, but you'll find it's eminently logical.

It's inevitable that people will want to talk about the rest of their lives while at work—after all, they spend so many hours there. Ideally, you'll be able to refrain from too much carryover into work because you'll be living it up in your off hours, with a full social world, so you won't need to try to create that missing dimension at work. Maintaining healthy, or even rigorous, boundaries is a good discipline to help ensure that you really do have a life.

So don't be the type who stays late because they have nothing better to do, the kind of drudge who spends hours wasting other late-working employees' time. Even if you succeed in creating an impression of the heroic worker by putting in so many hours, it won't get you very far. Managers know who's really getting things done, and who's just jawing.

Check Your Life at the Door

I've found that the most common—and self-destructive—workplace blunder is sharing your personal life with colleagues. Such openness is diametrically opposed to the concept of a Work You. It's crucial that you check this insidious urge, because once it gets going, it's a hard habit to break. And once you've mixed up your private and your work lives, it's extremely difficult to reestablish a truly professional persona. I tell people it's as if a baker mixes up the sugar and the salt.

It starts harmlessly—say discussing movies with coworkers. Before long, you're describing what you did each weekend,

"WHEN I WORK, I WORK; WHEN I PLAY, I PLAY."

That's a good, lusty motto. If you can live by those words, you'll have an enviable existence. How? One half of the equation pushes the other half onward; soon it's like a set of train wheels charging forward.

Here's how the "positive-feedback loop" works (to sling a little jargon):

▶ Do the things you want to in your off hours— seek and obtain gratification.

▶ This gives you great energy to apply to

including romantic exploits and family dramas. Soon everyone in the office knows what's going on in your life, and you hardly care that people overhear your phone conversations. Naturally enough, others start thinking of you as the harried mom, the single guy, or the coach.

Once this has happened, you've sacrificed much of your professional edge. Coworkers need to mentally adjust, to shift gears a little, when discussing business matters with you. Part of them wonders why they're going over a multimillion-dollar construction project with the eco-activist.

The tendency to mix work and outside life seems to be epidemic. Kathie Lee Gifford, for example, has been tormented

your work, and reduces, or even eliminates, the kinds of frustration that make people "act out" on the job.

▶ As someone who's on top of his or her game, you'll have an easier time getting good political results at work, because others naturally want to align themselves with someone like you.

▶ By handling your job skillfully—doing it well and ensuring that the interpersonal relationships are favorable—you bring that sense of mastery with you back out into the world.

▶ You'll succeed at doing and getting what you want in your off hours.

▶ And so on. . . .

in the press because of her obsessive habit of describing her children's lives in excruciating detail. Kathie Lee is America's example of what happens to someone's reputation when they bring their personal life to work. Maybe it reflects the lack of other forms of community in many peoples' lives. But work life isn't meant to be a soap opera.

Naturally, you will share some information about the rest of your life. Failure to do so would pique others' curiosity and imagination, and it would be a bizarre type of shutdown. Your human qualities are an important aspect of your workplace contribution. Anyone who's ever sat in on a meeting of high-powered marketing managers has witnessed a creative collaboration of brains, savvy, and, in all likelihood, very quirky senses of humor. In fact, your personality and outside interests were probably partially responsible for your hiring. Perhaps you noticed a tennis-racquet paperweight on your future manager's desk during the final interview, and mentioned that you also enjoy that sport. This mutual interest may have played a significant role in getting hired over several equally qualified candidates.

wrong turn! Seth and Tim both love *Star Trek*. Seth has a framed shot of the cast tacked to his cubicle wall and a *Star Trek* coffee mug. He'll gladly recount passages from favorite episodes with coworkers, but he makes it a point to keep these interludes to a minute or two. Tim, however, seems to have trouble distinguishing between his own life and the *Star Trek* universe. He wore Captain Kirk's uniform to the annual company party, for example, and tries desperately to be the office character. When Tim recorded a couple of *Star Trek* moments on his office voice mail message, his manager had to have a reality check conversation with him. But Tim will still reel off long passages with very little prompting, and coworkers tend to avoid him—especially Seth.

But it's crucial that you understand the distinction between personality and personal life—and keep your revelations about outside life to a minimum. If in doubt, it's nearly always wiser to withhold rather than to divulge. You don't need to seem robotic or uncivil. There are limitless topics and subjects about which you can converse without having to detail your own circumstances or life history. Everyone has seen hundreds of movies, for example, and it's one of the most pervasive sources of conversational energy in the world.

The key is balance. If you've recently had your first child, for example, then bonding with other mothers on the job is natural, normal, and generally worthwhile. But stop short of the others' interest level—let them come up to you with questions and suggestions, rather than draining the topic through your own Kathie Lee act. When you're mentally overinvolved with parenting at work, all the other parents inevitably will compare your level of professionalism to theirs in the same situation, and find yours lacking even if they were just as intense once upon a time. It also puts supervisors in a tough spot: It's difficult to avoid looking (and feeling) a bit like of an ogre when you ask a beaming dad to put away the 120 near-identical baby shots and get back to work.

If you have a prominent interest or hobby that you don't want to exclude entirely from work, then at least be certain to keep it in check. Don't let it take over more than a bare minimum of your Work You.

Through the Microscope: Corporate Culture

To derive a blueprint that will help you customize the Work You, you need to examine the kind of office or workplace you've entered. Is it formal or casual, open or closed, strict or loose? Ponder the following more specific questions to figure out what type of environment your workplace really is.

How many people come in right on time? It doesn't

matter what time the official work hours are, for instance, if the hours are from nine to five. What time do most people *really* get to work? Do the majority of people get in early? When they're late, what is the reaction of coworkers?

---

a shaggy dog story

I knew of an entrepreneur who ran a small music publishing company that was sometimes more like a kennel than an office. First, Saul, the company founder, brought in his own Labrador every day. Then he decided to run a recruiting ad in the local newspaper that read, in part, "Fun company, family friendly, dogs welcomed." A woman who leapt at the chance to have her cute little bichon frise with her all day applied for a job immediately. She was hired after a long discussion with Saul about dogs. A few months later, a young college grad came to work. His problem was that his roommate had an aversion to his pet snake. Saul told him to bring the cobra on in. Finally, a longtime employee's mother-in-law became ill and needed someone to look after her Rhodesian Ridgeback, Lucy, for a few months. You can guess where Lucy wound up. Most of the staff was fairly tolerant of this menagerie with the exception of one older woman who spilled coffee all over a silk dress when she tripped over Lucy, who had a habit of plopping down in the middle of the floor.

How does the workday start? Do people eat at their desks in the morning? Do they gather in the coffee room, or do they bring their cups to their desks? Does the work environment provide coffee or do you have to bring it in? Are they tea drinkers? Do they drink soft drinks or do they do nothing but start their job first thing in the morning? You can always tell what the work environment is like by what people are eating. Are they eating yogurt, cereal, bacon and eggs, Egg McMuffins? These are all symbols of what the company and the culture are about.

Does it seem to be a culture of single people or married people, or family people with children?

How do people dress Monday through Thursday? How formally are people dressed—that is, do the men wear ties? Do they have casual Fridays? Is Casual Day an important day?

Do people eat lunch at their desk or go out? What's the smoking policy? Is it a smoking culture or a nonsmoking culture?

Is it a pet culture? Do people talk a lot about their pets? Pets can be a surprisingly big part of an office atmosphere.

Is there a lot of interworker conversation? Do people have pictures, posters, or other personal items on their desks or walls? Do people smile much, or is the demeanor primarily serious? Do people gather around each others' desks or workspaces to share information (such as computer presentations)? Is there any playful flirtatiousness in the air? Do people look comfortable as they work, or tense?

What's the noise level? Do workers seem to take pride in their appearance and comport themselves with dignity? How do supervisors interact with their staff members? Does the company throw small celebrations for employee birthdays and such? Do employees seem to genuinely like their peers, or merely tolerate each other? Do people leave around five, or stay later?

How to Compartmentalize

Compartmentalizing is the essence of leaving your nonwork life at the door. It allows you to safeguard your privacy and protect your professional reputation from being affected by your outside existence.

But compartmentalizing isn't how most people naturally operate. The following suggestions address the main ways you're liable to let outside life seep into the work environment.

If the suggestions seem harsh, it's not because I recommend you become paranoid . . . well, not too paranoid, anyway. Most colleagues, supervisors, and subordinates doubtless are good-natured, trustworthy people, not enemy soldiers. But it's always smarter to err on the side of caution. Most people inject far too much personal life into their work sphere. Try to develop self-control: First establish habits of keeping it close to the vest, and then you can gradually, carefully open up in any given situation—but only as much as you choose to. The most successful executive personalities I deal with all have this knack.

Keep your personal trappings within bounds. Go ahead and hang some pictures of your family and friends, or a few tasteful art prints on the wall. But festooning your desk and cubicle with beer ads, psychedelic posters, or political buttons is another story. Minimizing clutter in general makes it easier to maintain boundaries, for a number of reasons: you're less distracted, and so less apt to let your guard down; there's less chance you'll accidentally leave out compromising information; and it reinforces your own professionalism, to yourself as well as to other workers. The pictures you display tell a million stories. People who have a lot of children but don't have any photographs of them send one message and people who have too many pictures send another.

I know someone who keeps a picture of Buddha on her desk, someone else who has a picture of St. Jude—all sending different messages to different people. Motivational slogans or sayings may inadvertently offend others. I guess there's nothing wrong with an occasional Beanie Baby, but the most important thing to have in front of your desk is a clock. Most employers don't provide you with clocks and although most people wear watches, I encourage you to bring in your own clock or little timer. (See page 203 for more on time management.)

Keep any wild information about yourself under wraps. People gossip, and even well-meaning coworkers are liable to share your information if it's good and interesting. So don't give them anything too juicy to work with. I'm always amazed by how much dirt my clients know about their coworkers, and I always point out that if they're not careful, everyone else will know just as much about them. It's smart to assume that someone in the vicinity of your cubicle is bored enough at any given moment to listen in on your conversation. This includes phone conversations.

Minimize personal phone calls. Always assume that some-one is listening to you on the telephone at work even when you whisper. As a matter of fact, the more you whisper, the more people will want to listen to what you have to say, and they'll make definitive opinions on you based on your personal phone calls. Your entire corporate reputation can be based on what people overhear about you in a workstation. There's no place for personal phone calls except for family emergencies. With the proliferation of cell phones and beepers today, take yourself into the rest room and make a personal call when you need to. Or have people call you on a beeper when they need you.

Master the art of artful vagueness. Even when someone solicits personal information, you don't have to play Honest Abe. If full disclosure isn't in your best interest, then hedge a little. For example, if two colleagues are boasting—foolishly—about how much they "partied" in college, and they ask you about your undergraduate days, you could say "I don't remember," and chuckle. You've participated in the spirit of the occasion without answering their inappropriate question.

Safeguard personal effects and documents. Don't leave such items lying around. They're too tempting—to thieves but also, more important, to snoops. People sometimes take their paychecks, leave the stub on their desk and forget that it's out. If you happen to leave a book you're reading on the desk, you can be certain that someone will take note of the title, and come to some conclusion about you based on it.

Nip it in the bud. It seems that nearly everyone messes up on this score: Don't get drunk with coworkers. Many workplaces, from parking garages to white-shoe law firms, include a culture of drinking. Colleagues go out on a Friday and unwind. Sure, you'll bond—and you'll also show or tell more about yourself in one evening than in an entire year of workdays. If you want to seem like one of the gang, stick to a single, carefully nursed drink. Once you throw back several, it's far too likely liquid bravado will shove discretion out the door. It's sad when I see professionals who work so hard to cultivate a professional image throw it away at the office holiday party by turning confessional, aggressive, lecherous, or whatever. The

Work You is based on regulating the truths about yourself you choose to present at the job; but alcohol is an indiscriminate truth serum, the all-purpose foil to a carefully built Work You.

Get the outside help you need. If your life hits a crisis point, there's a wealth of available assistance of which you can—and should—avail yourself: counseling, therapy, mediation, detox, support groups, trainers, confidants, and so on. Explore one or more of these avenues, but don't expose your problems at work or solicit personal help from colleagues. Don't deny or ignore the real situations in your life to the point where a coworker or supervisor has to approach you on the job to say that you obviously need to get some help. An important part of compartmentalizing is to take excellent care of all the outside components of your life.

This doesn't mean that you should try to deny your humanity. Even Mr. Spock would exhibit some signs of anguish if he had to weather a messy divorce. But make every effort to remain focused on work rather than on your personal travails while you're at the job. Eventually, you'll regain your emotional footing—and your stature at work will be intact. If it's absolutely impossible for you to maintain, then take some time off until you restore your composure. Even if you have to sacrifice some pay, it's a smaller price than to be permanently branded as fragile.

Outside affiliations—keep the emphasis on outside. The bonds formed through mutual interests, hobbies, sports, club memberships, religious organizations, and political organizations are profound. By all means cultivate and use them, but be thorough in drawing the boundary at the workplace. After all, the whole point of an outside connection is that you're free to explore it during your off hours. If you and a coworker friend discuss your mutual church activities, for example, in front of other employees, the only effect it can have is to distance them from you. They'll read your breaching of the private/public demarcation as a statement, a divider. Keep it low-key.

Also, appearing overeager to bond over non-work-related activities can blow your cool in several ways: it makes you seem desperate to connect; you appear uncommitted to work; and you seem shaky in the outside world as well, because you can't leave it where it belongs. If two employees discover a mutual interest in rock-climbing, and are excited as they share adventures and such, that's a lot different from two other workers who discover that they both root for the same basketball team.

Eluding Prejudice—The Ugly Truth

Though all of us presumably would want to eradicate racism, sexism, anti-Semitism, homophobia, ageism, and so on, they are still facts of life. Unfortunately, a lot of the "isms" are alive and well in the American workplace. Every year there are a few high-profile lawsuits against major U.S. corporations that have practiced overt discrimination. The best way to handle the work world is by adopting a low-key presence in these regards.

Obviously, I'm not condoning any of these ugly prejudices, or saying they shouldn't be resisted. I am saying that the workplace is not the best battlefield. I had one candidate, for example, who was a homosexual, and there was no question he was encountering unspoken opposition and disapproval that was holding him back professionally and leading to a lot of conflicts on the job. He adamantly believed that he shouldn't have to make any accommodation because of his sexual preference, and in moral terms, he's right. But in practical terms, no one was suffering but him. After several go-arounds with unsuccessful placements—he was actually a very gifted direct-marketing consultant—I finally convinced him to try a different approach, just once: To make a strong, sustained effort to tone down the flamboyance, so that all his coworkers weren't constantly forced to deal with his lifestyle and orientation. At the same time, I urged him to become actively involved in ACT UP, a prominent gay rights' group, as the appropriate forum for him to express and act on his anger at prevailing social conditions. This experiment was a huge success. He finally found a professional home where he could thrive relatively hassle-free, and he became one of the lead organizers at ACT UP. This was an example of someone finding a far better way to compartmentalize his life.

On the air my advice to listeners is this, "Why should your sexuality even come up?" In general, it's inappropriate to talk about one's sexuality at work whether you're heterosexual or homosexual; it simply should be a nonissue.

Other examples of workplace prejudice involve religious affiliation. I knew an extremely successful lawyer, a partner at one of New York City's white-shoe firms, as a neighbor for years, and I was aware of his professional prestige. Once I happened to bump into him on the street walking his children to synagogue during a Jewish holiday. I expressed surprise because I'd never known he was Jewish. He chuckled and said he doesn't make a big thing of it, that most of the other partners and associates at his firm don't even know. He commented that he considers it a private aspect of his life.

He's certainly not ashamed, nor is he trying to "pass." He works in a highly formal environment, where the lawyers very rarely socialize with each other, and it simply doesn't come up.

Another Jewish man who works at a company in Philadelphia called my show to share his experiences. Because of religious restrictions on the Sabbath, he has to leave work earlier than the other employees do on Fridays—especially during the darker months, when the sun sets early. In the past, he'd always thought his coworkers resented him, and he actually believed there was a taint of anti-Semitism in their attitude. So finally he spoke to the company owner and aired his concerns; the owner had no ready-made solution at first, but as the two talked it out, they both realized that the problem probably had to do with special privileges rather than religious allowances. This man's coworkers were bothered by the fact that he got to work fewer hours in total. It hadn't occurred to him to make up the hours at another time, but they both decided it was a good idea. He says that not only did the atmosphere change for him once he started coming in earlier one or two days a week, but a couple of his peers even sheepishly admitted that it had rankled them a little, but that they'd felt it would be trespassing on dangerous territory to bring it up.

Comfort Zones

Separating church and state is one big part of forming a successful Work You. But there's another side that's nearly as important: the necessity of leaving other people alone.

A workplace needs to be a comfort zone suitable for accomplishing the job at hand. This requires mutual consideration and an unspoken agreement to allow everyone else to concentrate. At MTV headquarters, a lot of tumult and adrenaline are expected and required, but at most job locations, people don't want their personal space—physical and mental—to be invaded. Your Work You should refrain from intruding on other people unnecessarily.

The main ways in which people impinge on each other involve: overstepping interpersonal boundaries, creating unwanted sound or noise, bodily presence (hygiene), broadcasting personal information, and inflicting views on others. These sins are all easy enough to avoid if you're aware of the ground rules I describe in the following sections.

Outward Boundaries

A basic principle of communication that's especially critical in the work environment is: Do not overstep the limits of propriety. A tactful person never invades someone else's privacy by asking questions that the other declines to answer, for example. The hail-fellow-well-met routine might fit well into a fraternity context, but not the workplace. Do you trust someone who starts calling you buddy after knowing you only a couple of weeks?

To avoid being an obnoxious presence, try tact. Let people reveal things willingly rather than trying to pull it out of them. Thresholds of privacy vary widely. The only way to be certain that you don't cross them is by sensing each individual's boundaries, not by pushing buttons until you hit a nerve but by patiently letting them reveal who they are.

Sound Pollution

Since the proliferation of the workstation/cubicle environment, more wrangles between neighbors involve sound than any other problem. There's nothing more annoying than unwelcome noise. At work, you need to accommodate the most sensitive common denominator. Not everyone will mind hearing you hum quietly to yourself all day, but some will, and it's for those coworkers that you need to adjust your habits. Other ways to soundproof include never chewing gum, or eliminating a nervous habit, like bouncing your leg up and down, if it creates a banging sound or sensation. Even throat-clearing, though it sometimes can't be helped, should be avoided. At least, make sure you're not continually clearing your throat. Most people find it annoying and grating even if they don't realize it consciously. Use lozenges, if that's what it takes (though be careful not to turn your lozenge-sucking into an annoying habit either).

The main sound bite gripe is simply speaking. Some people don't seem to realize that telephones are very adept at picking up sound, and that speaking above a conversational level is unnecessary. Your telephone speaking voice generally should be a little quieter than your normal expression, because the phone is an amplifying device. If anyone around you complains, chances are you've been bugging everyone around you. Whenever I've noticed that a candidate sounds louder than usual when we speak on the phone, I make sure to coach the person when they come to my office about this trait. One time, an executive assistant told me that a few people had complained about her phone-voice volume, but that she'd just ignored them! To those sitting around you, this is not a trivial matter.

The same goes with visiting other cubicles and entertaining at yours. If you're having a discussion, especially if it's not work-related, it mustn't interfere with anyone else's ability to concentrate. Also note that if you have any problem with hearing, it's your responsibility to correct it with hearing devices and special amplification on your phone; others shouldn't have to suffer.

Hygiene

It's extremely embarrassing to find out that you've given physical offense for some reason, and it's embarrassing when others do as well. The common goal for most offices is to keep things antiseptic. It's more than enough distraction to deal with messy interpersonal dynamics and power struggles without having to think about who needs to shower more often than they do. Part of the tacit rules of the professional workplace is that no one wants to be reminded that we're human animals any more than is absolutely necessary.

The main thing is this: Don't give offense. Maintain impeccable grooming standards, and if you have any reason to believe you have trouble with, say, bad breath, then practice extra diligence to manage the problem. Nearly all successful salesmen carry mints with them at all times (the "Altoids advantage" or the "Tic Tac touch"). How much does it matter? Some sales professionals claim it can mean the difference between getting by and getting rich. It should go without saying that you should never do anything at work that you wouldn't do in front of acquaintances (not only friends); if you ever see someone examining her hair for split ends, for example, this will probably subtly influence your opinion about her for a long time after.

wrong turn! Jennifer thinks the perfume she wears is on the subtle side, but she's alone in this opinion. Just a little of her favorite fragrance goes a long way, yet she slathers it on instead of dabbing. She's created a serious atmospheric problem for a few officemates over the years, but no one has had the heart to tell her— partly because Jennifer clearly thinks she's a class act and would be likely to tee off on anyone who threatens this self-perception. Whatever her other strengths or weaknesses as a worker, Jennifer is thought of as an odor first, and a professional second. Everybody shares the same sense of wonder: "How can she not realize?"

Now, most people who have poor hygiene or naturally smell more than others do not know this; even the closest of friends aren't likely to tell you if your dandruff is snowlike, for instance. So I recommend that you tell a couple of friends that this is important for your job—and that means your career— and that therefore they should pull out all the stops, that you can take it. (Then you have to live up to this promise.) It's far better to be told by a friend about your endemic sweat stains than to be known as the pit boss by your entire staff. Remember, smell is the sense that penetrates deepest. I've noticed that when a caller complains about a supervisor who has this problem, for example, it's the first thing they mention.

Another utterly inappropriate intrusion is any discussion

about bodily functions. This may strike some readers as ludicrous, and it should, because there should be no reason for anyone to be told that it's not acceptable to casually discuss these matters. Unfortunately, it happens all the time. Even if it's the office culture to openly discuss alimentary conditions, monthly cycles, or other aspects of anatomy and physiology: Don't! It's unprofessional in the extreme. Not only is it very likely you'll create a terrible impression among those who overhear, but it sends a base message to yourself about your relationship to work.

Personal Information

We all know people at work who seem neurotically driven to blurt out their opinions or experiences, sometimes at the most inopportune moments. These workers are considered unstable, and virtually never advance professionally. Just because some of your coworkers seem to get a kick out of your private-life tales doesn't make it okay to be the office raconteur. One of your peers who does not especially cotton to your tell-all style may get tapped for an important position that directly affects you.

A good policy is to provide information that someone requests, but not much more. This way, you keep your Work You free of bad habits such as boring people, bragging, and wasting time. This will help you avoid typecasting.

You risk bugging coworkers in a variety of ways by introducing personal dramas. First off, many people simply do not want to know your story. It's just bad manners to interfere with others at work. Coworkers may find it distasteful or even offensive to hear about your spouse's gallbladder surgery. It's a matter of context. Belching is fine in the men's locker room, but in the middle of your best friend's wedding it wouldn't fly. Every sphere has its ceremonial qualities, and most workplaces are fairly austere.

Also, people who habitually talk about themselves strike others as egotistical. When you gush about your seven-kilometer charity race, the quiet marathoner at the next cubicle can't help but snicker. And if you vent negativity, whether about your bad luck at love or a public figure you despise, it reflects poorly on you. If you're self-involved, and vocal about it, you'll forfeit some of the respect and trust accorded more discreet professionals.

Plus, you can easily sow resentment. By crowing about what a brilliant student your daughter is, you compel others to take a comparative look at their own kids, or at the fact that they're childless. And if you're foolish enough to spout off about sensitive subjects—politics and religion being the most obvious ones—you're going to put off at least some of your coworkers.

The worst violation is the one people seem to take the most pleasure in: discussing their sex lives. Among the many dangers associated with this subject is that if you go too far for someone's taste, you could be accused of harassment. The subject doesn't belong in the workplace—neither explicitly nor through innuendo. A person who needs to brag—or gripe—about his or her romantic escapades strikes most others as insecure and pathetic, and the employee might be making others feel terrible about what they're missing in life.

But this issue is not about to fade away anytime soon. Spectacular harassment stories at dot.coms have become frequent newspaper fodder, along with countless articles over the

cubicle reality   Robert and Jason worked at the same architectural firm in Chicago for about three years and were on friendly terms. Both men were homosexual and on Mondays they'd frequently discuss the cultural events they'd been to over the weekend or planned to attend during the week. They would also allude to their current romantic partners, in passing, and occasionally refer to parties and general wild times. Two recent hires happened to hold very intolerant feelings about gay people, and they were assigned cubicles close to Robert's and Jason's. Within two months, both of these new workers—one a woman, and the other a man—filed a written complaint with their supervisor, griping about having to listen to deviant conversations. Management was in a quandary. Robert and Jason were thoroughgoing professionals, superb at their jobs, and well-liked. Yet the two new hires were offended, and neither Bob nor Jason denied that they conversed about their love lives. In fact, discussions about weekend escapades are not acceptable. On the other hand, virtually everyone in the company agreed that the bottom line here was intolerance. Much to everyone's relief, the two offended parties left the company before long. But in the meantime, management reorganized all worker cubicles by function rather than accounts, and as a result Bob's and Jason's cubicles were no longer adjacent.

percentage of non-work-related Web surfing going on, and how much of that is porn-related. The fact is, America has a very strong puritanical (and litigious) streak; much of what is acceptable in, say, France (where most of the workers kiss twice on the cheek in the morning) would be a major court case here. The wisest approach, by far, is to play it ultrasafe:

Censor any impulse to blurt out an off-color comment, assume that whatever you say can and will be misconstrued, and never make a colleague feel sexually uncomfortable for any reason at the workplace.

Your Point of View

Nobody should have to deal with other employee's political or religious theories. Those are not issues that belong in the workplace—unless, that is, you work at a nonprofit organization or the headquarters for a sect, where such subjects are part of the professional vocabulary.

---

wrong turn! Alicia, who managed a telemarketing division at a New York City seminar management company, decided to put up in her office a poster of a controversial political figure whom she admired. When one of the seminar directors heard about it, he was highly offended, and told Alicia as much. She claimed the complaint was baseless, and they both were soon furious at each other. When the company president was asked to intervene, he insisted Alicia take down the poster despite her protests that it violated her free speech. Afterward, things gradually returned to normal, but the air was never truly clear again. There always lingered a whiff of strife from the unsavory incident. The problem would never have happened had not Alicia mistaken her workspace as a forum for her political views.

Verbalizing isn't the only way people get their viewpoints across. If you subscribe to a magazine with an extremist point of view and occasionally leave it on your desk at work, that lets everyone know where you stand. Arguably, that's not exactly imposing your perspective on your coworkers, but if it's left in the open, where most cubicles are situated, then it's not exactly private either. Just because it's your cubicle doesn't necessarily mean it doesn't intrude on others. For example, if you were to hang up a small image of a Confederate flag on the wall within your cubicle, that image will make a lot of noise. It's challenging for everyone to just get along at the job; don't be so unprofessional as to raise the bar farther.

The Work You Looks the Part

Your appearance plays a significant role in establishing a Work You. Your first goal should be not to stick out. Being a slob or an eccentric dresser calls attention to you for the wrong reasons. Workplaces are more conformity-based than the world beyond, and too many employees and managers seem to have little better to do than look for deviations in anyone's appearance. It doesn't take much—a trained office sniper will notice frayed shoelaces in a nanosecond. So you must be able to protect yourself from attack.

Once you accept and master the basic rules of decorum and dress, you can assert your originality and individuality. Within those rules of self-presentation, there is room to display some tasteful style without going beyond the pale. Try to be a little more stylish than your peers to help you stick out in a positive way. However, your emphasis should be on subtlety.

Don't Make Fashion Statements

Unless you're a performance artist, work is not the place for outrageous fashion statements. Your appearance should signify the following: I'm here; I'm capable; my eyes are on the ball; and I'm glad to be part of this team.

One caveat to this rule: I have done a huge amount of work in the design and furniture industries, where a somewhat higher premium is placed on personal style than holds true in, say, banking. Generally, in the New York City– or California-based visual image fields, a lack of flash is seen as a statement of sorts—an antistatement. In design, there are wider differences in attire from company to company, depending on the given firm's image, so I've seen literally every mistake in the book—candidates who come off as too flashy or too drab, too deluxe or too low-end. You name it. If I worked primarily with law firm executives, my understanding about appearance would be far narrower.

Don the Uniform

Every workplace has a dress code. At some companies it's more explicit than at others, but there's a set of accepted attire for each job. With a tremendous amount of flux happening in the work world at this time, it's more important than ever to be attuned to what's going on with dressing habits. To a certain extent, things aren't changing as much as the media portrays, but the fact remains that there is truly a "casualizing" of wear happening across the country. It's been building for a while, ever since the 1970s actually, and the dot.com movement has given it a big push. Until recently, this was merely a Friday-only phenomenon, but now a casual-wear policy often refers to the entire workweek. It all depends on the company and the industry—and on the economy, so don't be surprised if there's some backlash before too long.

Even old-line law firms have gotten in on the act—still requiring attorneys to wear suits to court, of course, but recommending that they go the simple slacks-and-shirt route when visiting clients. It started with the Silicon Valley lawyers, who needed to restore some sense of common culture with their start-up clients, and it has spread from there as more companies in more sectors are relaxing work standards. The firms want to avoid lawyer alert situations where the gulf between the attorneys and the client is too obvious.

---

wrong turn! Anne was an attorney in her mid-thirties who was returning to the workforce after taking time off to be a full-time mom. When she took a part-time job at an on-line game company, she was enthralled by its casual, open-air atmosphere—nary a cubicle in sight! Not only that, most employees were under thirty and seemed to pride themselves on being very cool. So Anne began sporting hiking shorts and sports sandals to the office. More than once, she commented on how liberating it was to be able to dress so comfortably after her years in city offices wearing conservative suits. She was making an enormous error in judgment. Her immediate colleagues, three other working mothers, found her appearance insulting and ridiculous. Her underlings found it difficult to take her seriously. Within a year, she was asked to leave.

If you're hired at a company that's adopted a casual-wear policy, that doesn't mean the code isn't just as precise as the old-fashioned two-piece-suit style; it just means that the particulars have changed. If you deviate from the company's norms, it will be noted, and probably with disapproval. Show up on a Monday wearing a three-piece Armani suit at Amazon.com, and your peers will be as incredulous as if you wore shorts to work at Goldman Sachs.

wrong turn! One young subdepartment manager at a research firm told me this amusing story: His division held Tuesday afternoon strategy meetings, which were attended by about seven managers. Usually, there was a lot of joking around, especially as the meeting convened. This manager said he and the company's marketing VP would often discuss a couple of CDs that they both held in high esteem; it was their little thing. One day during the summer, he showed up at this meeting without his tie on, because it was such a hot day. When the marketing VP asked him where his tie was, he thought the VP was kidding —after all, they normally chatted about Bob Dylan! But when the VP asked him for the third time in a row, he finally "took the hint." A little irritated, he went and put on the extra tie he kept at work. Afterward, the marketing guy took him aside and said, "You know, I was actually doing you a favor. It's okay for us to shoot the breeze for a few minutes talking about music, but if I'd let you sit through that meeting without a tie on, you'd have seemed like a joker, an amateur. Believe me."

What some people don't realize is that it's much more complicated to be a power dresser in a casual environment than in a formal one. In the past, a man would need a well-tailored, seasonally indicated, quality suit, good shoes, a high-grade light-colored shirt, and then he could improvise with interesting (though not flashy) ties. Now, however, that same male employee will need to coordinate more elements of color, material, and pattern to appear both professional and stylish year-round.

In your choice of clothing, quality, choice, and condition all count. The most important thing is that the items themselves, including their color, suit the context. Nearly as important is that everything look crisp. Quality, as in whether the garments are expensive designer wear or reasonably priced standard issue, counts most when it has bearing on the job, such as in high-level retail.

Footnote: Don't forget that footwear is an essential part of attire. Some people end up spending nearly as much on shoes as they do on clothing itself. They realize that the fastest way to size someone up is by looking down—at their shoes.

Shoes must be in good taste, good repair, and good condition (that is, shined). Nubucks, for example, are not suitable for formal work environments, nor are ankle boots for women. Shoes have an added dimension, in that if they don't fit right it doesn't merely look bad; poor-fitting footwear can make you irritable and cause you to walk oddly. Your feet are not to be trifled with.

Traveling Right

When it comes to traveling, many people tend to go as informal as possible, partly to make a business trip feel a little bit like a vacation. Basic advice is to bring along some wrinkle-resistant clothes, have enough variety in the types of garments to handle any contingency, and bring a nice blazer if there's a possibility you'll have to attend a cocktail party, for example.

Keep in mind that people who are wearing more businesslike, formal, or upscale clothes tend to get better service, whether at an airport lounge, restaurant, or business meeting. If several people are potentially getting bumped from a flight, the one who looks most official has a subtle advantage in getting the first seat that opens up. It's not unusual to hear stories about high-powered executives who were treated shabbily by service workers who didn't realize their status.

wrong turn! Here's one strange instance I've heard about: Glenda, an associate lawyer at a large firm, was attending an official social event with other members of the firm during the spring. She was wearing what she considered to be a dignified outfit—a blouse and a skirt. The next day, one of the firm's senior female managers told Glenda that one of the older male partners had asked this manager to inform Glenda that her attire had been inappropriate; specifically, he'd said her blouse had been somewhat see-through. Glenda was outraged at first, not only by the accusation itself but by the proxy approach of informing her. When she thought about it later, she realized the source of the problem was that she'd been wearing a very dark-colored bra, with a fairly light-colored blouse, and that's why it was visible. She was still irritated but being the professional she was, she merely made sure not to make this error again. She'd found out that her firm permitted very little leeway when it came to dress.

Sex Appeal

The issue of how women should dress at work is in some ways more complex than it is for men. There are competing pulls: the need to appear businesslike prompts many professional women to don the frequently unflattering, dowdy suits. On the other side, women who wear cleavage-bearing dresses and short skirts tend to be viewed as tarts. It's not the easiest balance. But I've found that women who make no apologies for their femininity tend to fare best in the work world. It's not necessary to downplay your attractiveness, though obviously tastefulness is of paramount concern. Many women I've worked with have found that reasonably form-fitting dresses have been great at work. The boxy suit look is the least appealing approach; better to go with attractive separates.

Beyond Clothes

Not only is the impression you create greater than the sum of your parts, but there are more parts involved than most people realize. The following includes the obvious and the less tangible elements that contribute to others' gut-level responses to you, both at first meetings and from continuing exposure. Some people become uncomfortable when I point out that these elements of their appearance really do matter, but this is how the real world works. When a caller complains that she thinks it's unfair that she's judged harshly because of her obesity, I offer some empathy—and then I recommend she join a health club. It's easier for her to change her body than for humanity to change its nature.

Attentiveness. Look into people's eyes when you speak with them. Anyone who tends to drift off, or seems drowsy, makes a bad impression at work. Everyone wants to really be listened to when they speak, and to be truly focused when they respond. If you can do this, then you can keep interactions brief without cultivating ill-feelings. A one-minute conversation or discussion with someone who is present is far more satisfying than a twenty-minute chat with someone who doesn't seem to be there.

Facial features. For better or worse, attractiveness counts. All manner of studies have shown that better-looking—and taller—people have a built-in advantage for getting ahead in life. If you know your best features, flaunt them! Just make sure not to be obvious, or the opposite effect will result. A man and woman with nice eyes is wise to wear contact lenses, for example, rather than glasses, and to apply perhaps a slight dusting of accentuating makeup. A man with dimples should smile easily.

Expression. Certain qualities can come across very clearly just from the way a person holds and moves his or her face: intelligence, warmth, wit, charm, kindness, edge, scorn, anguish, impatience, humor, and so forth. We all have acutely developed sensors for this type of communication; no matter how subtle, it registers. If your Work You puts people at ease and makes them feel good while communicating with you, then you have an immensely important advantage in the work world.

Energy. People with an optimistic, high-energy attitude tend to be liked. For starters, energy is contagious; studies show that when elderly people adopt puppies they do become more active. And even those who say "You're spunky; I hate spunky," are eventually won over by people with good vibes.

Voice and speaking style. We all know how strongly different voices affect us. People who speak too loudly make us cringe, while those who speak too softly make us impatient and irritated. Some people are too nasal, or monotonous, or overemphatic, or whiny, or any number of other distasteful things. But those with strong, varied, mellifluous voices and speaking styles can say nearly anything and get away with it. Your voice is such a powerful tool that if you're intent on attaining power in the business world, voice training is a very smart idea.

Hair. This is a big, important subject that can be examined at length, but I'll keep the discussion brief. What matters is neatness and a good style, as well as color and density. For men, baldness is not necessarily a demerit, but combing your hair over the patch is. And forget about toupees, which are probably the most ridiculous cosmetic invention in human history. Anyone who dyes his or her hair should be sure to do so thoroughly and whenever any roots start showing—in other words, if you do it, do it right. Trendy styles rarely make a professional impression. Whichever way you wear your hair, it's important to maintain it; have it cut and styled regularly, don't wait for it to start looking shaggy. It's also a good idea to find a style that works, and stick with it. Don't be afraid to spend money for a good hairstyle and color.

Facial hair. At most American workplaces these days, facial hair is in very short supply. Facial hair is one more element that must be scrupulously groomed, that forces others to work out their (often ambivalent) feelings over the subject, and that often looks just plain awful on people who choose it—retro, or sinister, or phony. Unless there's a compelling cultural or fashion reason, facial hair is best left out of the picture. I believe men should not wear mustaches and beards of any sort if they work in a professional environment.

And women with facial hair should think seriously about electrolysis or another removal treatment. It's not an easy thing to recommend to a client, but I've seen people's careers turn around once they took this step—maybe by coincidence, maybe not.

Jewelry. This must be low-key and discreet, not call attention to itself. Historically, the elegant string of pearls was one of the few jeweled adornments that was welcome in the formal workplace. That rule has loosened some, but not all that much. I love to see expensive jewelry on a woman in the workplace, but a boss may be intimidated. Don't wear it on the day you ask for a raise.

Tattoos and piercings. No one can decide for you whether or not to have tattoos, but I can tell you it's unwise to display such adornments at work (unless, I suppose, you work in a copy shop or video store). If you have several tattoos on your shoulders, then don't bare that area at work. The same goes for piercings—use your discretion.

Makeup. It should be neat, tasteful, and subtle. Cosmetics can be a strong ally, but if it's tacky, everyone notices— even men who are impervious to most fashion matters. If in doubt, get yourself an expert makeup lesson at a department store or spa.

Weight. Like it or not, obesity is a major turn-off in American society. It makes others think you don't care about your own well-being or have any self-control. Emaciated people also make others nervous, because they seem unhealthy.

Age. This is another unfair factor. Part of the current wave of antioldsterism is a result of the media hype surrounding the on-line companies launched by barely postpubescent pups, and some of this will die back down. The truth is, someone with experience is usually a much more valuable company asset, assuming they don't need to be on the technological cutting-edge. Nevertheless, without being overt about trying, you probably want to seem younger rather than older. Don't affect a ridiculous, inappropriate demeanor or dress style, but avoid stodginess. Notice what other people your age who look like they're on top of their game are wearing. Emulate elements that fit in with your own company's culture. And don't hesitate to consider plastic surgery. It can turn your life and career around.

Gait. The way someone walks tells people a lot about how the person feels about him- or herself. When people who've been perpetually out-of-shape start to exercise religiously, for example, their gaits often change, becoming more self-assured and springy. Try to be aware of how you carry yourself, maintain as strong and straight a posture as you can, and yes, it's very wise to get or stay in shape.

Handshake. While this isn't an item of appearance, it's an integral part of making a first impression, for men and women equally. The advice is straightforward: Your handshake must be firm, and you should look someone in the eyes when you shake.

Eating manners. You can't blame your upbringing for your table habits. By the time you're old enough to work at a professional job, you're responsible for having civilized etiquette. Some basics: Don't start eating until everyone at the table is served, don't talk with a full mouth, keep your mouth closed

WORK EAT-IQUETTE

While business lunches (and dinners) can be a mon-
umental waste of time, they're also the venue
where a lot of important relationship-building goes
on. Corporate meals entail their special brand of
savoir faire. Meals are an important forum for
interpersonal dynamics, and knowing how and what
to order is a sign of class. A well-played meal can
seal a deal, a client, or a job, so use them appro-
priately. The following menu of rules will serve you
well, whether you're eating with coworkers or
bosses, at work, on the road, or on an interview.

▶ Never be abusive to any wait staff while
dining, even if you receive the most appalling service possible. Everyone will know the service is
bad, and you come off a lot better by not making
a big deal about it.

▶ Do not drink alcohol, unless it's appropriate
—that is, unless everyone else is doing so, including the "guests of honor."

▶ Don't order special or extravagant dishes,
but don't order the cheapest thing on the menu
either.

▶ Never overorder.

▶ Don't pretend to know too much about wine
or extravagantly order wine.

▶ Restaurant selection should work in conjunc-
tion with the environment and the reason for the
meeting. Consider the restaurant's noise level if
you actually need to have a serious conversation at

this meeting. If you're entertaining a group of executives from the Midwest, for example, it might be unwise to take them to a restaurant that serves an especially spicy ethnic cuisine. Unless you know they enjoy Thai food, stick with meat-and-potatoes-type establishments. Ask in advance if anyone has unusual dietary requirements.

▶ If you're arranging the meal, and can afford the time, go early to arrange for the table that best suits your purposes—that often means one situated in a quiet part of the dining room, or a booth. Ask the maître d' for a larger table than you'll need, so nobody feels cramped. If this is obviously going to impose on the restaurant's business needs, then a generous tip is called for. Remember the table number for next time.

▶ Never act like a big shot in the restaurant. And it's not necessarily good when the people in an extravagant restaurant know you. (Just try asking for a hefty raise when your boss knows that you already eat a few echelons higher than he does.)

I read that renowned music lawyer Alan Grubman always picks up the check: "I always like people to feel obligated to me—whether it's my clients or the people I'm dealing with. Obligations usually make for a better deal," Grubman told *TALK* magazine. Grubman's right. I suggest following his advice, *except* when you are on an interview or with your boss. Then you should always let that person take the lead in picking up the check —although you may still end up picking it up.

when chewing, avoid slurping noises, be careful not to let food drop all over the tablecloth—or your own clothes, of course. This is stuff that everyone should learn in their families, but not all families share table manners that would make the grade in the work world. It astonishes me how many executive candidates eat like slobs when we go out for lunch.

The Watercooler Is Half Full

Instead of seeing the constraints of the workplace as something you submit to, focus on the upsides, the privilege of doing interesting and challenging work with people you respect (even if the work is sometimes tedious and rote, and some of your coworkers are duds). Instead of continually straining against a nonexistent bit, apply your mental energies to making your workday as smooth and interesting as possible, keep your senses perked for opportunities that might come your way, and look for more conducive environments if your current one is not satisfactory.

How Gossips Work

Whether or not you're personally inclined to talk about people, some of your coworkers certainly are—and you're fair game as subject matter. Forewarned is forearmed, so you should know how gossips work. The first point is that not all gossips are malicious; some people just take inordinate delight in discussing the lives, habits, traits, and fortunes of others, without any rancorous intent. The second point is that it's impossible to tell the difference between this sort and the malignant kind,

UNMOVING IMAGES

One reason people plateau out at their companies is that they've become trapped in their own self-created niche—as a particular "type." If you're known as the office workhorse, the most interesting, high-profile opportunities are likely to pass you by, despite the huge amount of effort you contribute to the company. If everyone thinks of you as the party gal, your name won't be high on the list of assistant marketing managers asked to participate in the budgeting process. The first challenge is to be aware of how you present yourself, the second is to be aware of how you're perceived, and the third is to change things if you don't like your "role."

Below are some of the most common designations to avoid, with suggested "corrective" measures for several of them.

▶ *The A**-Kisser (sometimes known as the yes-man or -woman).* Nobody likes or trusts a spineless toady, and they're often the first to get the ax when there's a changing of the guard. Realize that you don't need to flatter the big cheeses to get by; there are better ways to use your energy and talents. Besides, the honchos don't respect such fawning anyway.

▶ *The Doormat (also sometimes known as the yes-man or -woman).* No one takes this kind of person seriously, including the "benefactor" the doormat serves. Learn to stick up for yourself and

(continued)

have your own opinions. If your boss loses interest or confidence in you as a result of your burgeoning independence, then the alliance was a flimsy one anyway.

▶ *Good-Time Charlie (or Gus) or Party Gal.* Fun to have around, but not professional, good-timers seem to others like arrested adolescents. Learn how to behave with sobriety at social and official events, and start increasing the intensity of your professional activities.

▶ *Space Cadet.* Sometimes this refers to an eccentric, creative, or brilliant type who doesn't march to the same drummer as most of humanity. It might seem like a flattering reputation, but in truth it's a bad one, because space cadets have zero managerial potential. Come in for a landing, and try to assume a joint leadership role on a meaningful project.

▶ *The Kid.* This is a nice, comfortable niche when you're just starting out, because everyone thinks of him- or herself as your mentor and you have a lot of room for slip-ups. But if you're still considered "cute" years into your career, then you've failed to mature professionally. Try to connect with one mentor who can help you start to grow into an "elder."

▶ *The Joker.* Too much irreverence or wit is perceived as slacking, failing to take serious matters seriously. Leave the arched eyebrows and goofy faces at home for a while, and see how it affects your work life.

▶ *Superman* or *Wonder Woman.* These are sometimes polite names for workhorses, those incredible but self-effacing performers who never get the full credit they deserve. Start to make sure that you receive thorough acknowledgment for your contributions, and concrete rewards. Unless it would be way off base, mention to your supervisor that you wouldn't mind being given some credit in front of the other workers in the department.

▶ *The Cynic.* You might be right about the tawdriness of the workplace—or, indeed, of all humanity. But this doesn't come off as wise, only bitter and defeated. There's no upside, actually, to this stance. As long as you stay in the working world, you might as well make the best of it. And here's a true fact (not a satirical jab): A lot of cynics return to the human fold once they start a regimen of antidepressants. As an experiment, pick a small work project and carry it through with enthusiasm (even though it'll probably be forced). See what happens.

▶ *The Go-Getter,* or *Overachiever.* This would seem to be a great designation, and it often is. But such employees are sometimes perceived as being hypercompetitive and entirely self-centered. If you want people on your side, be sure to help others out along the way, and show some humility. For one week, make it a project to help out a different coworker each day—and don't tell anyone about it.

so treat all gossips the same—as potentially dangerous busybodies, connivers, and snipers who can't be trusted. If someone proves him- or herself to be better than this, then you're free to be pleasantly surprised. But don't let yourself be unpleasantly surprised: Protect yourself against them. Dealing with gossips exemplifies the importance of keeping your personal life personal.

Now, to be fair, I should say that my business would be a lot harder, if not impossible, were it not for the human impulse to spill the beans, share the dirt, or to be "in the know." That's how executive recruiters and agents get their best leads. There are people I value as much as police prize informers, except mine aren't intent on hurting anyone, but rather helping other people in the industry move forward (which in turn helps them out).

But the gossips I refer to here are the intracompany snoops and stooges. Don't feel that you need to ingratiate yourself with them or that they'll do you dirty. There's every chance they'll do you dirty even if you do ingratiate yourself, so it's a moot point. Just understand their modus operandi (as presented in the following) and proceed accordingly.

- ▶ Anyone who asks more questions about you than other people do should be considered a gossip (unless you're at a job interview).
- ▶ Anyone who's especially intent at hearing about your previous job experience, who you know, and what you think about people should be seen as a gossip.
- ▶ Work-related gossip is valuable, but what gossips really covet—and therefore the most dangerous mate-

rial of all—is information about your personal life. This is the area where gossips really specialize. In this way, they're similar to a restaurant: Food is its stock-in-trade, but its wine list is where it makes its real money. (And they both love to dish.)

► Gossips will not divulge anything substantial about themselves—though many are good at appearing as if they are. Gossips tend to be highly defended and have very thick skins, so don't think that dirt about them makes them as vulnerable as others would be. And malicious gossips are ruthless, which gives them an "advantage" others lack.

► Good gossips use assistants to gather dirt, so be careful about what you let your assistants know about you—and keep them happy!

► Gossips are very flattering, they'll make you feel funny, smart, well-liked, anything . . . so long as it helps them pry info out of you.

► Just because someone is breezy and up front about being a gossip doesn't mean they're harmless. It's usually just part of their pose.

► Be as vague as possible when replying to a gossip's probing. Waffle. Remember that gossips are very good at deducing, so even a little bit of personal information can kick the door open. Telling most people what neighborhood you reside in is no big deal, but revealing that info to a skilled gossip could be tantamount to handing them your bank PIN.

► As long as you're on sure footing about what you will and won't say, don't think you need to absolutely avoid gossips. Some are fun, and some can be useful to you even if you're not especially useful to them. Gossips respect people who are smart about when to be wary, but they'll continue to throw questions your way, so never let down your guard, not even after you've known them for years.

▶ Accurate gossip can be very helpful to you. Knowing that a coveted job is about to become available, for example, is a positive result of gossip. So don't entirely shut off to the gossip dimension, just keep it very low key.

▶ Though your close friends at work really do like you, the majority will still not be able to keep your secrets.

▶ One way to inoculate yourself against the truly vicious type of gossip is to not be implicated yourself. When you hear ugly things being said about other people, walk away. If you stay and soak up the prurient details, you're nearly as bad as the gossiper.

Where Do You Draw the Hemline?

I've been asked by many recruits, and even the occasional phone-in caller, about how to decipher a company's dress code. Usually, these hires are intent on assembling a wardrobe that will work best for them and also be appealing. My advice comes down to the following points:

▶ Start off conservatively. During your first few weeks or months on the job, take a low-key approach, and spend this time carefully observing the dress habits of coworkers. Observation of the boss is the first and best tool you have.

▶ The next tool at your disposal is inquiry: Ask your supervisor or a coworker about the parameters at the company. Don't pose the question to be about you but about the company—not "Would it be acceptable for me to wear . . ." but rather "Do any employees wear . . . ?" This way, you'll get more of an overview in the response.

▶ Do not be the one who tests the limits. Whatever the parameters are, don't push up against them. Don't be afraid to show a little imagination; just proceed very consciously.

▶ Dress as befits the tone of the company. Some Silicon Alley companies in lower Manhattan expect their executives to look like nightlife hipsters every day.

▶ Pay close attention to any comments you get about your appearance, especially it they're coming from your manager or others on that echelon, but your coworkers could also provide very helpful signals.

▶ Make sure you wear clothes suitable to your station at work. If you're an assistant at a company where the partners wear $400 outfits, don't wear a $900 Brooks Brothers suit. It's inappropriate for a variety of reasons, including: You're less likely to receive a decent raise if you present yourself as already flush.

▶ If your peers wear high-quality garb, then make that a priority for yourself. In those circumstances, it's much smarter to buy a few top-grade items than to buy a wider selection of lesser-quality pieces. Put aside some money to continue to build your wardrobe—and in the meantime, make sure you coordinate your dry-cleaning schedule so you're not caught flat. Think of the money you put into your work wardrobe as an investment with a high rate of return. If you're not sure where to shop, just ask a cohort.

Can You Relate?
Workplace Relationships

THE CRUX OF YOUR WORKDAY IS RELA-
tionships—with clients, supervisors, subordinates,
colleagues, and senior management. The majority
of questions I field from candidates, clients, and
callers to my show are person-to-person issues as
opposed to matters relating to company policies or
balancing work and domestic life. Most people
call in to complain that they cannot stand their
manager, they're being forced to deal with a coworker's neurosis, or endless variations on such
themes.

If you can get a handle on how to manage
different workplace relationships, I guarantee your
job satisfaction will increase dramatically. A pro-

fessional star, someone who shoots his or her way up the ranks in record time, always has the best grasp of human dynamics. Conversely, when employees have weak people skills, they often end up spending a lot of their time sorting out miscommunication and grappling with conflicts they helped create. They're not only less productive, they're miserable. So it's in your interest to study the workplace dynamics specific to your company, as well as to apply the general rules of good working relationships.

The Three-Month Rule

Certain approaches apply in any work situation, across the whole interpersonal spectrum. For example, if you're new to a company, or even to a particular department within the same company, take some time to figure out the culture— observe the prevalent dynamics. How outwardly friendly do the employees seem to be? How do peers interact among themselves, and how do supervisors/subordinates and employees in different departments communicate? For your first three months, focus much more on taking it all in rather than trying to become a full participant right off the bat. If you hang back a little while, paying diligent attention to everyone else, you'll probably avoid a few costly feather-ruffling gaffes.

Meanwhile, ask loads of questions. When you're new, there's really no such a thing as a dumb question. (Contrary to the common catchphrase, there is such a thing as asking a stupid question: It's when someone asks something that they really should know by then. During your break-in period, you're reasonably exempt from this criterion.

I'll never forget starting at Haworth, the Fortune 500 furniture company. I was the new kid on the block, coming in to a situation as close as any family. My boss was a friend of most of those he had hired. Our head showroom manager and the receptionist were cousins. Their uncle was our realtor. The technical support person was the showroom manager's brother-in-law. You could almost hear the theme song from "The Sopranos" in the background. The parent company in Grand Rapids, Michigan, had no idea what was going on in this division, but as the newest member of the family, I kept my mouth shut. I used my three-month rule to learn the ins and outs of the company, what was acceptable, right, and wrong. I observed who was responsible for getting my expenses paid, who knew the boss's schedule, who was the loudmouth, who was quietly competent.

Let others stumble first, find out who your friends—and enemies—are. Stay low-profile the first three months. In doing so, I wound up a cherished godson instead of exiled to Sicily. To this day I am still friends with that boss, and he is now a client.

Find Commonality

No matter where you work, you can uncover common interests that help you bond with coworkers. You don't want to spend too much time and energy bonding, but a little shared-interest camaraderie goes a long way. People connect over a huge range of interests: culture, sports, politics, spirituality, parenting, illness, exercise—the possibilities are endless. Sometimes people bring props to work displaying their outside interests (see Chapter 3); in other cases, it just comes up in conversation. If you overhear someone discussing an interest, it may not be appropriate to jump into the conversation, but it's acceptable in most cases to bring it up later: "I overheard you telling Rachel about seeing the Dalai Lama in Central Park; I'm interested in Tibetan culture myself."

way to go! I once placed an advertising account manager, Gerry, who told me that the comptroller at his new firm was an especially grumpy character, but he had enormous sway in budget allocations. One day Gerry noticed a golf magazine on the mailroom counter addressed to the comptroller. Gerry waited until he was in the elevator with the comptroller and then mentioned to another colleague that he'd happened upon a golf tournament on TV the night before, and it had reminded him that his sister had gone to private school with Jack Nicklaus's daughter. Gerry had learned a thing or two about the Nicklaus clan as a result. The comptroller's ears visibly pricked up. The next day, the comptroller stopped Gerry in the corridor and asked him about the Nicklaus connection. He was delighted to learn a few trivial details about the golfing icon's off-camera life. Gerry even brought the comptroller a color Xerox of a photo his sister had taken of the Nicklaus family at a school event twelve years earlier. Gerry couldn't care less about golf, but it was enough of an opening to establish a rapport with the lonely, curmudgeonly comptroller, and this stood him in good stead when budget time rolled around.

Establish Rapport Across the Board

At every company, it pays to have good relationships with as many people as you can, including those on the lower rungs of the company ladder. And not just the junior professionals— the assistant editors, first-year law associates, executive assistants. With them, it's obvious that some will turn out to be stars, and you'd be foolish to have snubbed them. It's wise to cultivate good relations with clerical and support staff as well.

Indeed, anyone can be a useful ally at some point, even the most unlikely people. I've heard about thousands of situations where a savvy receptionist or mailroom clerk saved the skin of a well-placed executive. In nearly all these cases, that executive later paid attention to the underling who helped them out. All it takes is a little bit of the common touch, an effort to treat everyone like a person, no one like a nonentity. Sometimes it looks silly or false, such as when you see a seven-figure-income investment banker talking basketball with the guy who sells newspapers in the lobby. But sports discussions are a great equalizer among males, and the connection is no less real because of the economic differences. I know of dozens of stories in which someone who wasn't highly educated but was actually very bright displayed an aptitude that helped them move ahead, and far exceed all expectations.

Everyone Needs a Mentor

Mentor is a funny, sometimes misunderstood, sometimes overused word. I can remember having mentors as far back as when I was twelve years old. My first mentor was Bert Steinberg, a local Armonk neighbor and a CPA, who helped me in a local youth committee that I headed. We were trying to get a teen center in the town of Armonk. Bert read about the committee in the paper, took me under his wing, wrote and edited all my letters to the town board, accompanied me to meetings, and was my first mentor.

Another mentor of mine was Dr. Max Link, former president of international pharmaceutical company Novartis USA and vice chairmen of Novartis Worldwide. He had earned

EIGHT THINGS I'VE LEARNED ABOUT MENTORSHIP

▶ You don't necessarily have to formalize the mentor/mentee relationship.

▶ Some of the best mentors don't know they are mentors.

▶ Mentors are cheaper than career coaches.

▶ It's important to know and grow beyond your mentor.

▶ Mentors can be relatives.

▶ There's nothing wrong with searching for a mentor. The best mentors start out as strangers and become close friends.

▶ Mentors may come from completely different backgrounds in terms of religion, race, and values.

▶ Sometimes you don't realize someone was your mentor until he or she is no longer part of your life and you feel inexplicably wistful.

THE GIFTS OF AGE

We're living through an especially acute phase of youthophilia, in which the worship of youth is at an all-time high in the business press, and college grads are commanding higher salaries than ever before. True, younger people are starting businesses at a faster rate than previously, but the statistical shifts aren't that extreme. Younger employees have always been ambitious, and have had the freedom to put in the hours required to make things happen.

But it's easy in this climate to forget that the best mentors are older. These workers are far more likely to be willing to spread the information and lore they've accumulated, whereas younger people are still trying to horde it in these hyper-competitive times. This isn't universally true, of course; plenty of older managers jealously guard their hard-won insights, and there are loads of open and supportive younger managers out there. But in general, the older ones will come through more readily with help, advice, corrective advice, and general support.

While you still want to hitch your wagon to the young stars, when it comes to intensive instruction, head to an old wise one.

multiple Ph.D.s and was by far one of the kindest executives I've ever known. He taught me you can be nice and still quite successful.

The best mentors are not necessarily formalized relationships. Your mentor may not even know that he or she is mentoring you. Mentors are usually, but not necessarily, older. They have usually achieved a level of success beyond yours. It's important to realize that not all bosses are mentors. Some, in fact, can work as almost anti-mentors. You'll know the difference because you'll feel it in your gut.

Work Friendships

Friendships are one of the great pleasures of working. Sharing collaborative challenges that involve discipline, creativity, and teamwork provides an ideal context to get to know people and bond with them. Inevitably, many of our best friendships were formed within the crucible of work. But as I've said before, the trick is to balance the professional with the personal—always with an emphasis on the first. In terms of friendship, it's inevitable that you're going to watch the backs of your friends at work more than you do for mere acquaintances. But you can't let that tendency get out of control and degrade into cliquishness, exclusivity, or the Blue Wall of silence. What you do together in the outside world is your business, but on the job, you and your friends are, fundamentally, coworkers. Don't lose sight of that.

This also means keeping a lid on the amount of merriment you share on the floor. Everyone in your department doesn't need to hear all about the great body-surfing you both found the previous weekend in Virginia Beach, where you went with the families. It's okay to mention, but you don't need to recount the events of the day with each other.

Your work friends are highly valuable as strategic allies.

You can't expect people you don't know to tell you about an interesting position opening up at another division of the company, for example. You'll look after each other's best interests, that's only natural. But the point is never to do so in such a manner that you appear to be ignoring or undervaluing your other colleagues' interests. It's a tricky balance, so you need to stay aware and keep tuned to any feedback coming from coworkers or managers.

wrong turn! Ben Rosen put up much of the capital and a lot of the business savvy to help found Compaq; Rod Canion was one of the cofounders, and was appointed CEO once the company was rolling. The two were professional allies and considered each other friends, but when Compaq hit the skids in 1991, the two men disagreed vehemently on how to allay the problems. Unable to find common ground, Rosen and the board gave Canion the boot—subsequent to which, Rosen's strategic plan boosted Compaq to the number one slot for PC sales. It took Canion years before he was able to be cordial with Rosen again.

On the job you're being paid to do something and you're expected to maintain a professional demeanor (as determined by company culture). You may want to spend a half-hour discussing your buddy's marital woes, but that has to wait for lunch, and lunch cannot extend for two hours just because the conversation is so important. If the friend beset by domestic troubles is a member of a project team you're heading up and has been unable to carry his share of the load, and therefore is jeopardizing the project, you have no choice but to replace

THE BONDS THAT TIE

The most common sources of personal bonding at work come down to the following categories, with a couple of examples for each.

▶ Material possessions: collecting guns or restoring Thunderbirds
▶ Sports: fan or participant
▶ Culture: *Star Trek* fanatic or opera buff
▶ Style: downtown hipster or country club denizen
▶ Alma mater: Oklahoma State or Rhodes scholar
▶ Language: conversational French or granddaughter of Polish speakers
▶ Community: urban neighborhood or gated suburb
▶ Heritage: second-generation immigrant or DAR
▶ Ethnic background
▶ Hobbies
▶ Second homes, vacation destinations

him. If he's a professional, he'll understand and not hold it against you.

That example, which is based on a radio-show caller's predicament, is a good illustration of how high the stakes can be and how knotty the problems that arise as a result of mixing work and friendship. One good way to avert possible conflicts is to discuss this issue explicitly with your workplace friends at the beginning of any mutual collaboration on the job.

Most readers won't face such high-wire situations, at least not for a few years. But this example illustrates the salient principle: When business and friendship conflict on the job, business trumps friendship every time.

Throughout my years in radio and television, working for small companies and large, I've taken pride in trying to make friends with both men and women. Shere Hite once told me that men and women are often afraid to become friends at work, which she thought was a shame. I took her words to heart and forged many friendships with women. One in particular I have known for over sixteen years, through two husbands and two children. Professionally, however, we have not always agreed. I think her methods are inappropriate sometimes and our styles are very different. I have felt that she took advantage of her position as a mother in terms of time and scheduling. I let business decisions rule over the friendship in such cases, and there were even periods we did not speak for three or four months. Ultimately, the friendship has survived, and professionally, we both have always ended up on top.

Manage Your Manager

Friend, client, and one-time job candidate George Kordaris, a vice president at Herman Miller, once said that the best way to deal with your boss was to manage up. Here are five steps to optimizing your relationship with a supervisor:

1. Observe and understand your manager's traits, values, and style. Know his family situation, eating habits, even religion.

Does your boss take care of business ahead of time or wait till crunch time? Does she get flustered or stay calm when unexpected problems arise? Blame others or take responsibility? Keep well-organized or waste time finding things? Is she willing to cut corners when it's expedient or is everything scout's honor? These are the kinds of things you should be looking for. The way to keep your manager happy will depend on how they like things done, and what weaknesses of theirs you can compensate for.

2. Devise a working strategy based on this knowledge.

Strategize. Once you know with whom you're dealing, you can devise an overall approach and specific techniques to deal with your manager's strengths and weaknesses. For example, if your manager is a bit of an absentminded professor, take charge of organizing your projects as soon as possible, so the supervisor knows it's not necessary to sweat anything when you're involved. If possible, even photocopy the papers that he keeps to track the project, and bring them to your progress meetings. By lightening the supervisor's mental burden, you'll be a star in his eyes.

3. Find ways to make yourself useful (this also means not making yourself a liability). Be low maintenance but high payback.

The best way to be of use to your supervisor, of course, is by doing a terrific job, which makes him or her look like an excellent manager and trainer with a sharp eye for hiring good people. (Even if none of that is true.) Remember that trying to become friends with your boss is not at all useful to either side;

keep it professional and cordial. Do the amount of work that's required of you and then let your supervisor know that it's done and that you had no problems. That'll satisfy her a lot more than if you decide to be a hero and take on unrealistic amounts of work, which you have to deliver long after deadline.

4. Maintain good communication channels with your manager.

To be effective in your job, you need to know your supervisor's short- and long-term expectations of you. If you stay on top of where your performance is on the expectation spectrum, then your performance appraisals should never hold any shocking surprises. Don't assume you must be a passive reactor to your supervisor's signals and actions. Be an active participant in the dynamic. You never want to stray over the line into pushiness, but in many cases it will be up to you to initiate conversations with a busy supervisor, who will then be most grateful.

5. Ask for what you want, but only after you've produced what your boss wants.

Broaching and discussing the issue of money isn't an easy thing for most people to do, which is why it's so important to have a method. You should have a list of accomplishments that justify your request for more money or a promotion: After all, I already handle most of the tasks associated with that position. Then practice delivering the request so it flows naturally. Be ready to do some horse-trading, because you're not likely to get exactly what you want, in which case you'll need to maneuver to get what you need. Whatever conditions and terms you and your manager agree upon, make sure they're put on paper;

it's not a bad idea to volunteer to do this transcription yourself, and then hand it to the manager for approval.

Loyalty!

By helping your manager, by looking out for him or her, you increase your value immeasurably. (Of course, always make sure you don't negate that by being a shirker, for example, or a loudmouth.) It's entirely justified to let a supervisor know what you did, as long as you don't go overboard in your presentation; put it in a matter-of-fact fashion, never with a "now you owe me" tone of voice. Remember, your manager isn't looking for a guard dog, an attack dog, a lapdog, or any other kind of canine.

And do not, no matter what, talk badly about your manager behind his or her back. If the person is a hateful tyrant, and everybody knows it, then you still had better not say so. (Your silence at times will do the job anyway.) It reflects well on an employee when she can keep her own counsel even when her supervisor is patently abusive. Stick up for your manager if others are bad-mouthing him; if there's merit in the slams, then point out some of the manager's countervailing traits or achievements. Find the balance between presenting a good character (that's what the loyalty represents) while not being encumbered by a supervisory albatross (don't think of or present yourself as the right-hand person to a weak performer or low-influence manager). Another reason to clam up with any negativity is that in all likelihood it'll get back to your manager by way of one office conduit or another.

It should be obvious that if you realize there's no hope

for a productive, respectful relationship with a given manager, then look actively for a reappointment within the company, or outside it. If you find a position elsewhere, and your company tries to retain you with a counteroffer, it's of course imperative that one condition is reassignment to a different supervisor. Don't be excessive in your explanation, just firm. The company's executives usually know when they have a dicey manager.

Collaborate with Your Colleagues

No matter where they work, people who can get along with their colleagues have the best jobs of all—they have trustworthy allies, people they can call on for the occasional favor (which they reciprocate whenever possible); plus, they have a good time during the day and don't go home with clenched jaws, craving hard drink to unwind.

If you don't get along with your coworkers, then your work life will be hell. Not only will you need to watch your back every second, but the resulting isolation will make you hate the job itself. I've spoken to countless people over the years, in interviews and as radio callers, who find their work lives absolutely destroyed because of feuds with other workers. I've also heard from plenty of managers bemoaning the poisoned atmosphere in the department that results from bickering workers.

It's very common to hear people refer to their work group as like family—as if that's supposed to be a good thing! Often it indicates that the person hasn't learned the lessons from the preceding chapter, and is intermingling her different worlds too freely, to the detriment of both her personal and professional life. At any rate, one resemblance to family is indisputable: You can't choose your workmates. You can't expect to love, or even like, all your peers, though it's great when team members have affinity for each other.

If you ask a hundred people what they really want in a coworker, about eighty-five will say teamwork. Teamwork is comprised of five basic elements, and you should shine in all five of them if you want to be a true team player.

1. Carry your weight. Do your job well and promptly.
2. Accept suggestions with equanimity. Don't be a prima donna.
3. Be fun to work with. Have an upbeat attitude.
4. Share credit. Don't try to hog the spotlight or split hairs over who did what.
5. Work with the leader. Don't buck or resist the lead person's authority. When you have suggestions, offer them in a helpful manner.

If you can get a handle on all that, you'll be a star, the kind of worker everyone wants on their team.

Gauge Your Coworkers

The first step to getting along with coworkers is the same as with new companies: Know who you're dealing with. When you're new in a department or company, keep your observational antennae charged at all times. Think of yourself as a cultural anthropologist. It's even a good idea to take notes in the evening (but don't bring them to work).

way to go! Jason, a manager I placed years back at an advertising firm, told me about a new assistant account manager. Roberto didn't just bristle when Jason oh-so-gingerly suggested his ideas weren't 100 percent on target, he visibly seethed. Others were also concerned, thinking Roberto might (a) blow a blood vessel, or (b) blow up the office. After a few days, he returned to normal, but it was nearly impossible to work confidently with him. So Jason had called Dianne, a colleague at a company where he knew this problem child once worked, to discuss the issue. She confirmed that Roberto was prone to scary reactions, but she told Jason that Roberto was actually very gifted; his was the mind behind a few of their most successful branding campaigns. Dianne also said, "Let me tell you a secret about Roberto. The way to get him to chill out is by telling him you think his idea is great, but that he can improve it. What he does is come up with three radically different ideas in addition to tweaking the current one. And at least one of the new ideas is always a killer. Trust me; try it." Jason applied this approach at the next available opportunity, and was amused to see Roberto pull back his head in a "Oh, yeah? Well, I'll show you!" attitude and go off to the proverbial drawing board, returning with two superb new ideas three days later.

At the same time, make plenty of inquiries, with care. When you're new, you can ask coworkers questions such as: Do you think it would be okay if I sent this report to Jackie? Would she mind? Chances are that the response will include plenty of other helpful information about Jackie's work style.

When you know the kind of people you work with, you naturally will adjust your style of communication to best suit their style. Some people don't want to know the background details: Just the facts, please. They're intent on getting on with the work, and you can spare the ornaments. With others, a conversational style is imperative; to put a request or suggestion too bluntly just jars their sensibility too much. And some people are so sensitive to the tone of voice of other people that you need to be very careful you don't let it run over the sides when you're in a foul mood. These are just a few of the issues that come up, and which you'll grasp through a combination of watching and asking.

Sometimes you'll know where a colleague worked in the past, and you might know people who know the person, whether your contacts are still at the same company or not. This can be a gold mine of information, because your out-of-company contacts have less at stake. When someone is proving to be incompetent or uncommonly hostile, some discreet inquiries into their past often uncover a pattern of such habitual behaviors, and sometimes a solution to the problem.

Oil and Water

Even if a set of colleagues disagree with each other on fundamental matters of human existence and think each other's children are uncommonly ugly, they can work together perfectly effectively if they keep their eyes on the prize, trusting each other in a work context. This means that they're all professional enough to segregate nonwork issues and deal only with their shared mission: doing a good job together and helping their company survive and thrive. If everyone stays oriented in this manner, it's amazing how attainable fundamental harmony really is. I've dealt with numerous position candidates who came from backgrounds that predisposed them to think unfavorably about different types of people but who overcame such prejudices through work exposure. In fact, working with people you otherwise wouldn't get to know is one of the most progressive forces in our society.

way to go! The day Linda started at a small graphic design firm, the first thing she noticed about her officemate, Morgan, was the photo of Morgan shaking hands with Ronald Reagan. Turned out Morgan was a rabid Republican and had even worked on Reagan's presidential campaign. Linda, on the other hand, was a "tree-hugging, granola-eating, former hippie" from Berkeley, California, according to Morgan. The two circled around each other for quite a while, sure they would never get along. But they had the sense not to even try to discuss politics. Gradually, a funny thing happened. Forced to work on several projects together, they found they had a growing sense of respect for each other's professional skills. Linda was really good at project management, while Morgan was the company's creative spark. They also shared a healthy sense of humor, which turned into the glue that kept their working relationship together. After a few years as colleagues, they actually started their own company as partners. No one who knew them both could believe it, but they've been in business very successfully now—through two presidential campaigns!

Your coworkers are like members of a platoon. Even if sometimes you hate each other's guts, you still have to trust each other for your mutual survival, so you always come through. What this means, in the work concept, is that you:

- ▶ Communicate honestly and fully with everyone who needs to know certain information,
- ▶ Weigh obligations to different peers equally rather than pushing projects pertaining to people you like to the front of the line,
- ▶ Never speak ill of other workers on the job,
- ▶ Always listen to what your peers have to say, and
- ▶ Look for ways to remedy conflicts rather than escalate them.

It's not always easy to get along with others at work, and sometimes you have to bite your tongue till it bleeds. The most helpful advice I can give is to adjust your attitude in a manner that facilitates cooperation and agreement. Your current coworkers may be your managers, subordinates, or even business partners down the road. Today, your career is your current job. Tomorrow, your career might still be your current job, but with some of the positions and players rearranged. Treat every coworker with an eye to the longer-term possibilities. Don't blow up any bridges.

Dealing with Difficult People

Many seemingly difficult people are in inner torment. Even if they take out some of their anguish on others, it's a drop in the bucket compared with what they themselves go through. There's the phrase about not judging someone till you've walked a mile in their shoes, and with many bitter coworkers you really would not want to trade places for even an hour. Knowing this can help you maintain compassion. Sometimes people are experiencing terrible trials outside the job, and this

HOW TO DEAL WITH
A BACKSTABBER

Some people are hard to get along with because you're so different from them. But then there's the other type—the truly nasty rats. Without wasting time going into their psychology, I'll just make some straightforward suggestions:

▶ *Steer clear.* Try to have as little to do with them as possible. Unless you have credible reason to believe they're redeemable, don't accept any "peace offering" lunch invitation from them, because it's just a snare to find out some more

inevitably carries over into their work existence. It's not professional, but it is human, and if you were in their situation you'd also want to be cut some slack.

Many aggressive people are just trying to subconsciously protect themselves from being attacked first. They could have had a lot of bad experiences that have tilted them in such a manner. If you can muster up the patience and tolerance to put up with them a little while, they may come around—and end up being stauncher allies than you'd ever have expected.

Think of these difficult people as teachers in disguise. More than one spiritual leader has told adherents that our growth comes from our trials alone. After all, it's easy to get along with your friends; even when you run into some turbulence, the bottom line is that you like or love each other and

damning info. Give them a wide berth. And try to remove them from your mind as well, because such people are a drain on your attention.

▶ *Don't engage them in snipery.* Think of back-stabbers in this way. Don't let them pull you down morally. Be direct and terse in your interactions, and betray no sign of irritation; don't let them see it if they get to you.

▶ *Shore up your alliances with others.* The best way to control potential damage caused by a vicious coworker is by doing an excellent job and maintaining good relationships and communication with your supervisor and other peers.

have a relationship together that's worth salvaging. But it takes true patience to deal with people you fundamentally don't like. Those are the relationships and situations that strengthen our fiber—professionally as well as morally.

If you're thin-skinned, it's wise to learn how to thicken it somewhat. The work arena is a place of great tension and drama, and under such strains nearly everyone will snap from time to time. If you take these affronts personally, work life can be brutal, and one incident often spirals into many. But if you don't take these words spoken under stress personally—and remember, the choice is yours—you leave room for a speedy return to cool. When someone is nasty to you, it's always their problem: If you haven't harmed them, then they're behaving viciously; if they believe you have caused them offense or harm, then the only reasonable approach would be to talk it over with you rather than lash out.

When people are nasty to me in business, I try to abide by a very firm rule that is always the same, for men and women, for subordinates, bosses, and peers: It's imperative that you call someone on their nastiness. You should almost embarrass them in asking why they are nasty in specific, humble, and human terms. (Notice I am not recommending you ever return nastiness.)

Here's an example: I'm working with a recruiter in my head-hunting business. She suddenly snaps at me and makes a really mean remark. I know she's had a bad night, bad week, business is tense, we're under the gun, but the remark seems almost personal. So I turn to her, look her directly in the eye, and say very quietly and calmly, "Why would you speak to me so meanly? What's your problem?" If she looks at me and just rolls her eyes or is silent—a typical reaction—I keep pressing her to answer me out loud. I repeat, "What's the matter? Why did you say that to me? What's going on?"

Dare to ask people to their face if they don't like you. Dare them to tell you they have a problem with you. Make them say it, put it on the table. It's essential. Getting them to acknowledge that you know their attitude is mean is the only way to neutralize the situation. It works!

Avoid Discussions of Salaries

I've always been amazed at how much trouble results when people are foolish enough to go into salary issues with their coworkers. Even if it's someone in another part of the company: *Do not discuss what you or anyone else gets paid!* Don't go there with your close friends either. How much money people earn is inevitably a huge source of friction and resentment. It's probably more acceptable to discuss your sex lives with other people (though not at work, never at work) than to get into the dollars and cents of take-home pay.

Why shouldn't you do so with your colleagues? For starters, it may be against company policy. Just about every business expressly forbids employees to discuss pay with other workers. Not only does it sow dissent within the organization, but it's also sensitive information that a company wouldn't want its competitors to know.

There's no upside to sharing this information. When one side feels they don't make enough, they feel enraged, bitter, hurt. And the other party rarely feels good about it. When someone finds out about an inequity between his pay and another's, that doesn't water the garden so much as it plants seeds of doubt. It's poison. Once salary is out on the table among department or company workers, the air is infected— and it's extremely hard to kill the bug.

Say you and Charlie are work mates, collaborators, fellow microbrew drinkers, and both fans of the Red Hot Chili Peppers. Well enough and good—it's a wonderful peer-to-peer work relationship. One Friday after work you and he throw back a few Brooklyn Lagers at the local bar, and you bring up salary because you're planning to speak to your manager in a couple of weeks and ask for more money. So you want to know where you are in the scale. Charlie tells you what he makes— five grand more than you do! And there's no chance you'll get that kind of raise. So on Monday, Charlie is no longer your work buddy and ally; he's the overpaid bastard who wastes your time discussing music! Get the picture?

All I can say, over and over again, is *Do not do it!* If you feel you need to know what's fair pay in your field—let's say you have an upcoming performance review and you want to have a significant adjustment made to bring your pay in line with industry standards—there are countless other ways of finding out that don't involve your coworkers. Trade magazines print this information, at least once a year, and usually more frequently. If there aren't copies around of magazines serving your industry sector, then contact one or two and buy a reprint of the relevant issues. Or call up a recruiter and ask about the range. If you're that curious, there's a pretty good chance you'll be wanting their services before long anyway.

Office Romance

I've almost never worked in a company where I or someone I know wasn't romantically or sexually involved with someone else at work. There, I've said it. It's true. Sex at work is rampant. I'm not speaking of sexual harassment, but of pure, old-fashioned romance in the office. We spend so much of our time at work, we're so vulnerable while at work, it just makes sense that romance blooms, and sex follows. Actually, it's often more lust than love.

Think about it. How many couples do you know who met at work? How many times do you hear friends saying that they have a crush on someone at work, or that they'd love to date their boss? It happens everywhere—big companies, small companies, men/women, men/men, women/women. It happens in the boardroom. It happens in the washroom. It happens in the showroom.

---

you decide! Kathleen was on her second marriage and had two children when she was hired as an editor at a regional magazine. The publisher, Ross, was also on his second marriage and had four kids. With a reputation as a womanizer, it didn't take long for Ross to start flirting with Kathleen. Others in the office, including the art director and the editorial assistants, didn't take it too seriously. So everyone was spellbound the day Ross's wife stormed into his office, ranting about his affair with Kathleen, how despicable he was. She then announced she was leaving him that minute, and indeed moved into her art studio. It took the magazine staff, especially Kathleen, who quit immediately, a few months to recover from the turmoil this scene created. It took Ross and Kathleen even longer to get divorces from their spouses and marry each other. But that's just what they did—fifteen years ago. They now have eighteen grandchildren between them and are as happy as newlyweds.

The problem isn't sex at work. In my book, sex at work is fine. But talking about it is wrong. I believe in a "don't ask, don't tell" policy. Of course, sexual harassment is completely taboo, and should never be confused with mutual, voluntary office relationships.

I remember the days, when I was a teenager, working in the furniture store and suspected that one of the top salesmen was having an affair with one of the women at work. It was a small town, and one day I happened to be driving by the Ramada Inn. I was pretty sure I had seen both of their cars. Well, by now you know how I love gossip, so I called the hotel. One of the individuals was listed under his own name and he answered the phone. I quickly figured out he was with the woman. He was married, and she was divorced. Although I was shocked at first, I came to the realization then that sex and work are inseparable.

Whether office relationships are fleeting affairs or lead to marriage, there's nothing wrong with thinking of work as a potential arena to meet your mate or sexual partner, as long as you follow certain guidelines once you meet that person.

If at All Possible . . . Resist!

The Rule of Rules for office romances is: Be careful! This doesn't mean that you should skulk around in stealth mode, although there are times and places where that's advisable— and a lot of people seem to enjoy that aspect of on-the-job affairs. What being careful means here is to venture into these waters with open eyes. You'll know your eyes are sufficiently open if it stings a little to see the picture. You see, more is on the line than meets the eye. Even if a relationship works out beautifully, it still generally imposes strains on the participants' work lives, and involves anxieties and limitations others don't share.

And if a relationship goes bad, what's on the line isn't merely broken hearts and hurt feelings. Your professional cred-ibility is at stake as well: the respect you elicit at your company, and your extra-company reputation.

I happened to hear about two architects, both of whom I knew personally, who had started to cavort around the drawing board. They were both very intense people, people who had their amps turned up to eleven all the time, and my first response to the news was "Uh-oh!" Less than a month later, the male of the duo gave me a call and wanted to set up a meeting, just because he was "curious about whether there are any interesting opportunities out there at this time." Before I finished shaking my head in wonder, I got another call . . . from the woman. "Steve, I need to speak with you. I'm in the market for a new job, and I'm in the market in a big way!" Neither one of them could stand the sight of their company's building, let alone the sight of each other.

One last thing: The same cautions absolutely apply when you're on a business trip with a colleague. Don't do it for casual gratification, figuring no one will know. You two will know, and the liaison is likely to lead to an ongoing connection. It might not seem like such a big deal when you're on the road, but offices have a magnifying glass–like effect.

Discretion Is the Best Part of Valor

It's always wise to keep your love affairs as low profile as possible. The gossipmongers will have a field day when they find out about your love life, so it behooves you to keep it under wraps for as long as possible.

Some of my advice about compartmentalizing obviously goes out the window once you're having an affair with a coworker, but you should still try to maintain some boundaries. After all, your personal life still isn't everyone else's business. Proceed at work as if you're merely very good friends, people who have lunch on a regular basis and communicate well. Restrain yourselves from public displays of affection— definitely! Even couples who have been married ten years should refrain from PDAs in the work environment.

Some companies make it clear that interoffice romances are acceptable and permissible, as long as nobody's professionalism is compromised. If your company has a policy against such relationships, then be ultra-careful. In my experience, people tend to find prohibitory policies make it even more exciting. Even at companies where they wouldn't be fired, some workplace lovers find the hush-hush phase loads of fun, and highly romantic. Personally, I think it's likely your secret is open knowledge, and if so, the sneaking around bit is moot.

wrong turn! Max was the charismatic headmaster and founder of a small private art school. Single, thirty-something, and very good-looking, he naturally attracted a number of his female students. He was always careful to avoid encouraging them, knowing what a can of worms it would be. Then came Claudia. A smart, mature, gorgeous senior, she proved irresistible to Max. That summer, instead of going on to college, she married him. When word got out, his enrollment dipped precipitously and he was barely able to keep the school afloat. His reputation in the community was tarnished as parents felt they couldn't trust him. On top of all that, he and Claudia couldn't overcome the age difference and split up after a year and a half.

A love relationship between a supervisor and a subordinate is always a terrible idea. In fact, many companies expressly forbid this sort of affiliation, just as many universities don't permit professors and students to become involved. Once people know about a relationship between a manager and a reporting worker, everything is suspect: Any positive feedback, promotions, or other favorable treatment for the underling will be seen as favoritism, even if it's completely legitimate. Plus, the power differential puts the junior person at a horrible disadvantage professionally. (It's not too good for most relationships either.)

---

wrong turn! I heard a story two years back about Tim and Carla, young programmers at an established Silicon Valley firm who fell in love while compiling UNIX code. They frequently had to stay late at work on a special project. One evening they found themselves the only people left on their floor, and they decided it would be a novel idea to get amorous—"It'll change our whole perspective about this place," Tim suggested. Well, they were wrong about being alone; they'd forgotten about one conference room where an account executive had been quietly working on a sales presentation. Finally finished, this executive flung the door open, eager to get out of there, strode into the main office gallery, and. . . . You can guess what he saw. Tim and Carla were both fired the next day.

Why and how can you be sure all your romantic socializing is done outside the office?

Do yourself a favor and think of the workplace in an antiromantic context. Even if you and your love met there, and you're very grateful to the company and to your profession, change your perspective so you place a premium on getting out of there to be with your partner. This will help you establish some crucial boundaries. Make sure work is only about work. This way you're more likely to have a life; don't gyp yourself out of all the lovely experiences that people who don't work together get to have: meeting for drinks, going to cultural events together, getting dressed up. Don't let the fact that you work together rob your relationship of splendor. The best way to make sure of this is to cordon off the workday as a time when the two of you will deliberately frustrate your urges for mutual intimacy. Give yourselves a reason to stay as efficient as possible. This also pays off in terms of public perception.

One simple technique that helps ensure that the two of you will work-when-you-work-and-play-when-you-play is to avoid joint projects. If it can be avoided, don't collaborate on the same tasks, programs, or assignments. If such interaction proves especially pleasant because of each other's company, then you're likely to spend more time at work involved in the project, or else spend a lot of your nonwork time "processing it." And if the collaborative work goes poorly, that can be disastrous. Don't risk it. If you really need to see how you two work as a team, then take an extended vacation together, or raise a puppy (certainly before giving parenthood a shot). But don't make work the testing ground for your relationship.

Public Knowledge

Most of the time, it's obvious when coworkers hook up. When two people become lovers, nothing they do together looks innocuous any longer; they can't help it. So if you're sure no one knows, you're probably wrong. If you think no one knows, you're definitely wrong.

If you've both succeeded at maintaining professionalism

for a full year, say, then you may decide that the coast is clear, no one will hold it against you once they see that your work hasn't been compromised.

Or else, you might bump into some coworker or coworkers in town, and you'll all know that the jig is up, that it would be absurd to ask them to keep it under their hats. Once the story's out in the open, don't change your behavior. Don't be ruffled, and don't let your guard down. Just maintain. Slowly, over some time, you two might become more relaxed in the company of your coworkers. But if you undergo a sudden transformation, it'll make your comportment prior to your discovery seem less professional in retrospect.

Who's It Gonna Be?

Maintaining a relationship at work is somewhat like newlyweds moving in with one set of parents. It might be all right for a little while, but it's generally in the couple's best interest to find another living arrangement—sooner rather than later.

When people become seriously involved at the workplace, it's often wise for one of the lovers to find another job, either within the same company or, preferably, elsewhere. Obviously, this is no indication of failure or weakness, but rather a desire to secure both professional and personal happiness.

Sometimes this works out very smoothly. If one of the two people wasn't happy at the current job anyway, the relationship is another incentive to move on (as paradoxical as that might seem at first blush). But most situations are rather more complex, and the point shouldn't be who values their job less but rather what will be the best solution for both parties—and "best" includes the absence or minimization of resentment.

Typically, the more senior of the two gets to remain, but that often works out in a sexist fashion, because in most cases I've seen the male is the more senior; now that's changing, but the point is that seniority alone can't be the only gauge. An accomplished manager might be in a far better position to snag an even better job at this point in his or her career, whereas the less professionally advanced partner might be better off staying at the current company to accrue enough experience and knowledge to be optimally marketable.

It's smart to start discussing this issue early in the relationship, before the situation hits a critical stage. One couple I know met when they both worked on the West Coast for a $4-billion-a-year furniture company. She was married but in the process of getting a divorce. He had never been married. She was a manager, and he reported to her. Around the time they became romantically involved, she was offered a substantial promotion to become the regional sales director for the New York territory. She left California for this new position, and he followed shortly thereafter. They continued to work for the company, but she had a far more lucrative position and seemed to be the rising star. When her divorce was complete, they married, and she asked me if I would help her husband find a better position with another company. I was able to place him within a short period of time, and his career has been on an upward swing ever since. She is now the mother of two, happily raising her children full-time at home in Connecticut. While they met on the job and were never officially discouraged from working together, they found it better to separate their professional lives in order to grow as a couple.

SURE WAYS TO GET FIRED

▶ Keep a copy of your résumé in your company computer.

▶ E-mail or solicit jobs on your company computer.

▶ Send follow-up letters to a new prospective employer using your current company letterhead.

▶ Box your boss into a corner about a raise.

▶ Offend your boss's spouse, partner, or children.

▶ Be a high-maintenance employee (as discussed on page 42).

▶ Lie on an employment application. This includes things like education and previous work experience. It always catches up with you, not necessarily in the beginning of your career, but sometimes in the course of your working for a company. If you're caught in a lie, you will be fired.

▶ Be chronically late for work.

How to Cope If the Relationship Crumbles
Unfortunately, hearts get broken, often two at a time. What people need to do when they're racked up from a failed love is to put some distance between them and their partner, not to be forced to see them all day, every day. Many times, one of the members will depart, sometimes both.

But it is absolutely essential that when you enter a relationship at work, you prepare yourself for this possibility, and that you make a solemn vow to yourselves (and to each other) that you'll comport yourself with dignity and professionalism no matter how much it hurts. If you can't do that, or aren't willing to, then you probably have no business starting this adventure in the first place. Because the rancor, bitterness, rage, and destructive impulses can be abominable, and if you or your ex acts out, it can spell professional disaster. Again, I've seen it happen, numerous times. At minimum, it's smart to try to transfer elsewhere in the company if it's at all possible, so you don't have to have salt rubbed in the wound all day long.

And in the future, try to hook up with one of the hundreds of millions of people you don't work with.

5

There's No Such Thing as Small Talk: Communication

COMMUNICATION, IN ALL ITS FORMS, is the heart and soul of work life. Everything you say on the job has an impact, even if it's only subtle. All the components of communication have an effect: how much you express, the way you put things, and of course what you actually say. All of these add up to the overall impression others have of you.

In business, there is no such thing as small talk. Each time you express yourself, you have the possibility to influence perceptions—about you and about the situation at hand. Face-to-face conversations are the essence of office communica-

MORE TO IT THAN MEETS THE EAR

Most employees don't realize how many components are involved in strong communication skills. It's not enough to be able to express yourself clearly; true communication skills encompass all of the following:

▶ *Keen listening.* Pick up on nuance. If you let people talk, most will eventually tell you absolutely everything you need to know——their fears, sources of pride, weaknesses, and strengths.

▶ *Attentiveness.* This is the visual equivalent to keen listening: Maintain eye contact, for example, and don't fidget.

▶ *Selectivity.* Just because you know something doesn't mean you should express it. In general, you should say a lot less than you know. So even if you already know about the marketing department's plans, the point is to hear the department manager describe it in his own words, not to let him know that you've already caught wind.

▶ *Directness.* Nobody should feel as if you're wasting their time, beating around the bush, or trying to bamboozle them.

▶ *Tact.* Direct doesn't mean blunt, abrupt, or

tion, whether they take place at lunch, in a meeting, by the watercooler, or brainstorming in someone's cubicle. It is primarily through conversation that your office identity is forged. But when you deal with the outside world, the telephone is toe crushing. Just because "it's just business" doesn't mean people stop having human feelings.

► *Eloquence.* A silver tongue can help tremendously in charming someone.

► *Earthiness.* In some situations, flowery talk would come off as false; a down-to-earth style is what works. In union negotiations, for example, you probably wouldn't want to sound high-handed if you're taking management's position because that would only fan antagonism.

► *Delivery.* One's tone of voice has at least as much impact as the actual words. If you convey dire news with panic in your voice, then your audience will become very anxious; but the same news delivered calmly and with self-assurance can prepare a group to take constructive action.

► *Humor.* People remember your message when you also make them laugh.

► *Body language.* This can override everything else. If you're pretending to encourage an employee you despise, the way you hold your body can give the game away. If your arms are tightly crossed, for example, that worker will sense your antipathy is stronger than your positive message.

key. An effective phone manner is subtly different from a face-to-face style. The same thing is true of voice mail messages, e-mails, memos, reports, and presentations. Every form of communication has its own dynamics, and each communication is influenced by the other party or parties. The better you understand how communication works, and can put that into action, the more effective you'll be.

We all know people who are graced with communication abilities. Some are truly eloquent, while others are merely glib. But even the glib ones tend to do very well in the world of work, especially if they have strong political instincts to accompany their expressive flair. These high achievers understand how much every comment, conversation, or speech can count if you play it right. Most of them have made a study of communicating; it's not just natural skill or intuition. They know that even chitchat has a huge impact. When you read the memoirs of master negotiators—whether in business or in high-level politics—they all make the same point: "We appeared to be chatting about soccer, but what we were really discussing was the balance of power in the Western Hemisphere! We were jockeying for power, but cloaking that in a chat about soccer."

Fortunately, just about anyone can strengthen his or her communication skills. It might take practice, or even outside tutoring, but it can be done. I know from personal experience, because I used to have mild panic attacks before any public speaking situation. I got that tendency under control eventually by applying some focusing techniques. Nowadays, I can go on the radio without even a blip in my heartbeat. The panic was just a habit—a bad one—and nearly any bad habit can be broken. (The same is true of stuttering or mumbling or any of the other woes that make communication so hard for some people.) And most good habits can be learned.

It's also possible to learn to write clearly if you put some effort into it. Maybe you won't become the next Hemingway, but you can certainly upgrade your memo-writing techniques so they're concise and hold the reader's interest.

To master communication, you need to grasp two basic elements: quantity and quality. "Quantity" means knowing how much to say—and whether you should say anything at all. None of the top executives I've ever met are blabbermouths. Some are garrulous, but none just blurt and babble like many of the rank and file seem to do. As for "quality," that means knowing how to put things just right: how to express ideas clearly, directly, with just the right spin, and without causing unintended offense.

Choose Your Shots

When it comes to quantity of communication, I find that just about everyone overdoes it. They talk too much about themselves and reveal all their weak spots without anyone having to ask. Or they talk trash about coworkers, and demonstrate to everyone that they can't be trusted. Many intraoffice feuds wouldn't take root if there was less unproductive communication swirling around.

When someone shoots off his mouth, very frequently he ends up shooting off his foot as well. Badly timed or aimed communication is at the root of most workplace hassles. It takes many forms: a worker deeply offends her manager inadvertently by belittling a movie critic who happens to be that manager's husband; another employee tries to appear impressive by revealing an upcoming business move to one of the firm's clients at lunch; one worker tells two people in his department that he takes an "antidepressant cocktail," which, he claims, is aimed at treating all his particular mental problems. In all these cases, the employees would have been much better off if they'd kept their mouths shut.

Younger workers generally have more trouble knowing when to just be quiet. And that tendency seems to be getting more pronounced. I think the hypercompetitive spirit is putting tremendous pressure on young workers to prove themselves—to show that they have brains, nerve, talent, or drive. Combined with that is a sense of entitlement that comes from a very strong economy. Those just starting out tend to assume they know more than they do because times are good and they were able to land well-paying positions. So they immediately start spewing their point of view when given the opportunity or when they can shoulder their way into the center of a discussion.

This is bad style, and poor strategy. It's fine to engage in conversation, but the fact that you're at work should be in the front of your mind. And in a work context, you end up gaining more respect and political power by showing some restraint in your expression.

Why Less Is More

Words are a little like toothpaste: You can always dispense more, but you can never take it back. Also, a little goes a long way. That's why it's wise to err on the side of discretion in your work communications. I'm not saying one needs to be reticent

SELF-FILTER

This less-is-more approach isn't like taking a vow of silence. I don't recommend that anyone renounce human speech; far from it. Just learn how to filter what you say. It's a lot better to screen questionable comments before you say them than to impose damage control afterward.

For anyone who hasn't developed this brand of self-control, it will probably take some concentrated practice. But it's worth it, because with a little practice you'll have a strategic tool at your disposal forever.

Here's an exercise that will get you started: For one full week, pause before you say anything at work, maybe for just a moment or maybe for a while longer—it depends on the immediate situation. If your boss asks you about a spreadsheet, you'll probably have to answer right away or appear to be out to lunch. But during this week, you'll probably seem just a little odd to coworkers —a little too thoughtful, perhaps. It's an acceptable price for what you'll gain.

During that pause, try to quickly ask yourself a few questions. Select from the following (especially as it would be quite a feat to ask all of them at once):

▶ What do I gain from saying anything at all at this moment? Would there be any consequences to remaining silent? Any potential benefits?

(continued)

> ▶ Is this a tactful statement?
>
> ▶ Can it be misinterpreted?
>
> ▶ What is my subtext here? (For example: Perhaps you're making a snarly remark about an annoying software glitch, but what you're really saying is that technology nerds need to get a life.)
>
> ▶ Am I revealing more about myself than I need to or than I want to? What influences outside the immediate situation are affecting me? (For example: Perhaps you're mock-griping to your supervisor that you "never get to write the fun reports," but this is exactly the pose you struck as a child when you tried to manipulate your parents.)
>
> ▶ Is there a strategically smarter comment to make instead?

It's a lot to run through in your mind, but our brains work incredibly fast and it's surprising how much you can process in just a couple of seconds. The point of doing this for a week is that it should start to become a habit.

During this exercise, pay close attention to how people react. You can't compare their actual response against theoretical ones, but you can gauge whether your modifications are having the effects you foresaw. Perhaps there's a woman in your department who's religious, a churchgoer. And when she asked you a question about a project you replied that it's going "as well as could be expected" rather than saying, as you normally would, "it's even more of an albatross than we thought it would be." You adopted a gentler, more accepting tone. And as a result, you saw she seemed more comfortable than she usually does when speaking to you. Now, making that same accommodation might have had a very different result with your manager: "Don't give me that vague rubbish! How much of a disaster is it turning out to be?"

I guarantee you'll learn ten times more about workplace communication during this week than during any other. You'll discover a lot about yourself, about your coworkers, and about the nature of communication. How you use that knowledge is up to you.

or hold back when he or she has something valuable to offer or a question to ask. Rather, I'm cautioning against the tendency, which is widespread, to talk for the sake of talking, which is one of the worst habits in a workplace. Sure, there are situations where you'll gain influence by displaying wide knowledge about a subject. But just as often you'll merely get on people's nerves if you spout off.

Obviously, you need to be low-key when you're new to a job or company. Coworkers can't read the intentions behind your words yet, and some people instinctively jump to the worst possible conclusion. Plus (to make this critical point once again), it's always a bad move to reveal compromising personal information that colleagues can use against you.

Moderation in the amount you speak confers multiple benefits:

▶ It reduces the chance of saying something regrettable. It's one of the laws of physics: Anyone who talks a lot eventually will offend someone. You don't want to ever offend someone by accident; if it's intentional, that's another story.

▶ If you don't really know your subject, it lowers the risk of saying something foolish. Usually, people who talk excessively don't really have that much to say; they're just yielding to neurotic tendencies. Eventually, they say something idiotic.

▶ By regulating your verbal output, you can make your words count more. When someone speaks constantly, we tend to gloss over whatever they're blabbering about; it's all one big (and sometimes annoying) flow. But when someone who tends to stay on the quiet side pipes up, we pay close attention because the person's more of a mystery to us.

▶ Here's another way of looking at it: Books are designed to include a lot of white space, because that makes the words and images stand out. The same thing works with verbal communication. In conversation, writing, or presentations, leave some white space —room for people to ask a question or two. If you try to smother a topic by covering every angle, you won't wow your audience so much as confound them with the overload.

▶ When you talk less, you tend to observe more. There

are times to hang back and gather information; people who talk incessantly have a lot of trouble doing this.

The *New York Times* Rule

To some, the concept of discretion is too nebulous. After all, it's a highly subjective, relative term. You might want something more concrete to work with. In fact, I know a very tangible gauge you can apply.

A number of years ago, one of my own employees had created a few minor problems because he spoke his mind too freely. I suggested that he try to tone down his remarks, to be more discrete. Specifically, I told him, "Don't say or write anything you wouldn't want to see attributed to you on the front page of the *New York Times.*"

Of course, no one will be able to satisfy this rule 100 percent of the time. Sometimes during the course of doing one's job it's necessary to break it; for example, if your boss asks you, in confidence, to divulge something you've overheard that pertains to her, it's often politic and right to impart the info. But the rule should serve as a compass whenever the impulse to pass something on arises—when you feel the urge to vent, dish, or cut someone down to size, just think of how it would look as a headline. Most of the time, it would look petty or silly or, if what you have to say is outrageous enough, suitable as a headline in the *National Enquirer* instead. Had Disney chairman Michael Eisner adhered to the *New York Times* rule, I'm sure he'd never have called Jeffrey Katzenberg a midget.

The point is to get the spirit right. It pertains primarily to

ANYTHING YOU SAY CAN
AND WILL BE USED
AGAINST YOU . . . SOMETIMES

When it comes to what you say at work, a little healthy paranoia is in order. There must be something about being at a job that brings out primitive behaviors in some employees, because I've seen too many extreme examples to pass it all off as "just one of those things."

I recommend a dose of self-protective paranoia to everyone. No one reads you your Miranda rights when you show up in the morning, but it's still true that "Anything you say can and will be used against you" . . . sometimes. You're never speaking off the record when you're on the job.

Here are two prime examples where employees thought their communication was safe and later found out it wasn't. The first is when two good friends at work have a falling-out. The second is when no one seems to be paying attention.

When people at work forge friendships, there's loads of opportunity to get to know each other

bad-mouthing other people or your own company. Simply don't talk dirt about people; don't say anything that could be quoted out of context to someone to make you seem like an adversary. If you have an aversion to another worker or to your supervisor, you don't need to say so out loud for others to hear. You can say it with a shrug and some subtle facial expression. That's not

well. They go out to lunch together, shoot the breeze in the coffee room, walk around after work, and so forth. And they tend to share all the secrets and events in their lives; it's only natural, right? Well, natural or not, it's unwise. Because frequently enough, good workplace friends have a serious falling-out, whether or not it's related to work. It happens all the time. Sometimes the friends reconcile; sometimes they don't. Some people comport themselves honorably in such situations, but others become vengeful; the degree of affection they had turns into an equal amount of loathing. The personal information the two shared became available to all. The former friend knows just how to push the other's buttons, and uses this storehouse of information to do so. Some of the ugliest work situations arise between two former best friends.

The other situation is where coworkers register no response to what you divulge. They seem to barely take it in, and so you think it's safe to keep talking. Well, they're taking it in all right, and you shouldn't be surprised if down the road that privileged information becomes an open secret.

quotable in a newspaper. It's like telling the truth—by doing so, you don't have to remember to whom you told which story. And by not making hostile comments, you don't have to worry that your slurs will boomerang. You won't have to expend much energy sorting out friend from foe; you'll know who your enemies are, but they won't know that you're one of theirs.

The Gossip Paradox

When it comes to the *New York Times* rule, it would seem that gossip is a straightforward no-no. Obviously, it wouldn't look too good to see you quoted on page one as the source of information about two covert office romances, several doctored expense reports, and one "absolutely brain-dead" senior manager. Gossipmongers don't have the best reputation for professional behavior.

But gossip is something of a paradox because it plays an important role in the office information ecosystem. It's actually very important to one's future growth in a corporation. Remember that gossip is usually true, and in business knowledge is power, so you wouldn't want to be out of the loop. Even personal gossip helps you understand coworkers and managers—what their vulnerabilities are and what they like or dislike. This is invaluable information that can make your communications with them far more strategically meaningful.

The secret is to act as if you don't like gossip, and definitely don't be one who spreads it around. Usually, the people who are busted for gossiping aren't the real perpetrators.

Of course, as a headhunter, gossip is my stock-in-trade. In fact, the *New York Times* rule is the ultimate case of "do as I say, not as I do." My profession as an executive recruiter is virtually based on violating the rule. It's my job to know the inside scoop on all the companies and people I deal with: who's hired, who's fired, who's looking, who isn't, what company is on the rocks, what division is about to be canned, what bosses are clashing, who's having affairs with whom, and so on.

I need to hear the dirt, because I don't want to shepherd anyone into a bad situation. This means I solicit and listen to innuendo, rumors, gossip, rants, gushing, harangues, and a lot of other over-the-top communication. Of course, I always consider and weigh the sources. And in turn, I share only what's appropriate to any given person at any given time.

But my case is special. Smart company workers tread carefully around gossip, but they have a couple of reliable sources that keep them abreast. Again: Sometimes the only reliable source of truth at a company is what the workers are telling each other. Companies aren't teams or families; they're money-making entities. And managers and executives aren't usually inclined to let the rest of the staff know one iota more than is necessary to keep them contentedly toiling away. If the company is about to be sold, and half the jobs eliminated, top management isn't going to let you in on this rather pertinent fact; but the employee pool might already be sharing job leads with one another. Individual gossips have their value as well. The down side is that if you don't feed them anything, eventually they won't give it up to you.

Don't Be a Reactionary— The Twenty-Four-Hour Rule

Controlling your self-expression is never more critical than during a personal assault. Sometimes a guided missile can come at you with little warning, launched by a nasty coworker or destructive boss. It might take any number of different forms—blame for a flopped project, criticism for your quality of work, an accusation about cost overruns, and so forth. Not only do you have to deal with it, but it's also extremely important you do so without going haywire and making a spectacle of yourself.

These situations are where you find out exactly how well you've learned how to control your impulses to express yourself, because chances are you'll want to go ballistic on your antagonists. It's absolutely essential, however, that you not do so. Once you swing over into irrationality, you're thoroughly at the mercy of your attackers—and they will probably be disinclined to show any mercy at all. If you start to yell, or curse, or even threaten someone, you've blown it in a big way. Even if you're 100 percent right, the way you handled it isn't.

But your rage might be too overwhelming to calm yourself down and express your thoughts in words rather than squeaks and grunts of fury. No one can tell you not to have an emotional response, but you must get a handle on the nature of that response, and take appropriate measures to protect yourself.

The first, most important thing you must do when you've been assailed and are in a state of fury is . . . nothing! Do *not* take any action. Do *not* write a memo. Do *not* call on a manager to resolve the dispute. Do *not* do anything about what just happened. If it's close to the end of the day, try to make a fast getaway, right at five (not before, or else you'll appear to be too flustered). Go outside for a walk if you can. Try to get out of the office, even if it's just for half an hour. In the heat of the moment, it's best to do anything other than take immediate action. Try to think through the situation calmly; as soon as your heartbeat picks up, turn away from it temporarily. Figure out an approach for the next day (or Monday, if this was a Friday calamity).

While you're cooling off, take notes to help organize your viewpoint and plans. Some of the basic questions you should be asking yourself are the following:

▶ Was the incident truly as serious as you think it was? Is it possible that you misread it, or took a comment too personally because it hit a nerve unrelated to the immediate situation? (Ask yourself this set of questions a few times. Once you take action at work, you expose yourself and whatever issues you've brought to the situation.)

▶ If it really was a serious affront or a professionally damaging incident, does that mean you have to respond to it? There are two parts to this. First, will you potentially gain a strategic advantage by doing nothing (and thereby show that you're too solid to be addled by someone else's nonsense)? And second, do you want to put any more of your energy into this situation? It's a form of defeat to succumb to someone else's agenda for your attention; just because you have a boss who's freaking out about some imaginary problem, for example, doesn't mean that you have to buy into her hysteria.

▶ What kind of follow-up is likely on the other party's side? In general, you don't want to engage in conjecture, but here it could be useful to delineate what could be happening behind the scenes. Because if this attack is a calculated one, you might be appalled when you find out what machinations have been at play, and probably still are. You want to have some self-fortification to face whatever's going on behind the scenes, but at the same time you don't want to escalate the situation by imagining worse scenarios than the actual one.

▶ What are your options? Try to step out of yourself. In other words, if you were watching someone else deal with your situation, what steps would elicit your admiration? What about doing something counterintuitive? For instance, if you'll be attending a meeting with your attacker the next day, you could throw that person off by being in a positive, friendly mood, and making valuable contributions that win over the attendees. (Just don't appear to be trying too hard. This is an advanced-degree-level maneuver.)

▶ Are you prepared to deal with the situation without losing your cool? The answer better be yes.

Use this chill-out-and-strategize time to discuss your situation with a friend or mentor. Another option is to try to enjoy yourself as much as possible—living well is the best revenge. Try to adopt a wide-angle perspective and view the situation at hand as a game of sorts. Twenty-four hours later, you will be better prepared to respond and your day will likely go a lot better than it would have had you taken impetuous action the day before.

Put It Just Right

Knowing when and how much to communicate is fundamental to your survival and success in the workplace. Just as important is knowing how to express information. In fact, that is the essence of communication. In the rest of your life, how you express things is geared to building and sustaining personal relationships and pursuing your interests; at work, the how is aimed along a different type of trajectory: Your intention is to do your job as effectively as you can but also to increase your stature, build alliances, insulate yourself from attack, and move upward. At work, communication is fundamentally a strategic tool.

It's vital that your style of communication doesn't trip you up, that it doesn't create unnecessary problems. So you want to avoid ambiguity and indirect communication, because those qualities are the causes of so many problems. Instead, you want clarity and directness. That's what virtually everyone else wants too, because they allow the organization to function smoothly. But it's crucial to temper your directness with tact so you don't seem like a steamroller in a cornfield.

That combination—directness and tact—will make you an effective employee. But to be someone special, another ingredient is needed: spin. That's the ability to use information in a way that serves your particular needs. Spin can be subtle or it can be muscular, depending on the situation and on your own personality. It's not what you say—always—but how you say it that makes a difference.

Direct Does It: Why Being Direct Is the Only Way to Go

The keys to good communication are clarity and concision. Conversely, the enemies of positive communication are evasiveness, equivocation, vagueness, and any kind of dishonesty. Clear speech and writing are expressed in an unembellished, consistent fashion. You don't take five sentences to say what you could in two. In fact, obscurity usually is a cover for someone who doesn't really know what he or she is talking about. By getting straight to the point, your meaning is obvious, and if you're mistaken about a matter or need to learn more, that's clear as well, and you can get on with the correction or the education. There's no need or room for messing around when directness and clarity rule the day.

You don't need to hoard what you know. Knowledge is power, but knowledge begets more knowledge. By sharing your knowledge freely, more information will flow your way. When you're straightforward and forthcoming with your peers, you have a right to expect, and if necessary demand, the same in return. (Of course, you also keep your eyes open, and if there's a snake in the grass you don't take your boots off to give it a better shot at you. So, if a conniving coworker wants information you have in order to gain an advantage over you . . . no way.)

And what kind of information do you and your peers seek? Information that's actionable, that bears a direct relation to particular goals, that includes instructions on how to apply it, or that at least solicits their feedback. A clear, well-defined plan, with a timetable—for a book project, for example. A buying schedule for wood purchases to keep the furniture manufacturer supplied.

Misunderstandings are the enemy; ambiguity creates problems. If an assignment is explained poorly to a worker—let's say the worker isn't sure whether they're supposed to function as the production coordinator or managing editor of a new magazine project—that person can waste a lot of time pursuing the wrong goals and employing the wrong tools. This is profoundly unfair and dispiriting, and it's enough reason by itself to be certain of accuracy and thoroughness.

The best way to be sure all is clear is to have the other person repeat the information back to you. It's not always prudent to tell someone to regurgitate what you just told them, but there are more indirect ways of soliciting it, such as asking what order of operations they think they'll follow, "just so I know how to plan on my end." Or ask them if there's anything you've left out. If you are uncertain about whether everything is explicit enough, put it in writing, and if possible "cc" a third party as insurance (though not as a veiled threat). This follows the same principle as distributing notes after a meeting—it ensures that everyone's on the same page.

A Little Tact Goes a Long Way

Being direct and clear isn't the same as being blunt and tactless. A certain amount of politesse is involved in all communication, particularly when we're after a particular result. Sometimes being direct means allowing a bit of time for ice breaking. If not, the directness might backfire, alienating the other party rather than engaging them.

There are situations that are implicitly confrontational—for example, asking an employee why she missed a deadline, or conducting a disciplinary meeting. Any negotiating situation has an element of confrontation. Win/win is a nice phrase, but it's mostly an empty buzzword for what always has prevailed and always will: We have our side, you have yours, and we both want to maximize the benefit to ours without being so inconsiderate of yours that you won't want to do business with us. Many books have been written about negotiating tactics, which run the gamut depending on the context and the issues on the table. (In some cultures—for example, Japan—directness is not an acceptable approach.)

When a conversation that ought to be cordial disintegrates into rancor, that usually means both parties were miscommunicating. Once a situation has become purely confrontational, it's usually best to call an armistice and agree to reconvene later.

But the goal is to avoid such an outcome. You should always pursue a healthy directness, one that avoids nonproductive confrontation. Here are some key dos and don'ts to accomplish this end:

- ▸ Don't launch into your topic without any preface, which could be a benign comment.
- ▸ Do listen with full, thoughtful attention on the other person. Paraphrase what they've said.
- ▸ Do make your own position clear. Sometimes a sentence or two to establish your own stake is needed for context.

▶ Don't cut someone off in the middle of a sentence unless there is no other option. If you're in a terrific rush for another appointment, and they're talking a mile a minute without any pauses, sometimes the best move is to gently tap their shoulder and then tell them you need to leave but you want to set up a time to continue the conversation. The danger in these types of situations is that the other party will feel embarrassed, then ashamed, and then angry with you for causing those feelings. It's the badge of an excellent communicator when someone can handle these moments smoothly.

▶ Don't ask leading questions, because they insult the other party. Yet sometimes it's important to avoid point-blank questions too, in which case leading-up-to questions generally work. And those queries shouldn't be too indirect either. For example, leading-up-to questions might involve first asking about how much time remains before a deadline, then inquiring about the number of people working on the project, and then asking whether there might soon be a need to reallocate some extra help. A leading question would be more like: "Do you think you'll be able to triple the pace at which your team has been working, or should I plan on sending some of my people to help you out?" You get to the same place, but by avoiding an affront to the other's dignity the proper result is far more likely.

▶ Don't raise your voice. Ratcheting up the sonic assault virtually ensures confrontation, because Americans react to heightened decibels with adrenaline. (Some other cultures work by different rules.) Also avoid speeding up your speech, as is common when people become unnerved or impatient, because it compounds the communication obstacles.

▶ Maintain a pleasant disposition. Unless it's inappropriate, a smile makes a big difference in interpersonal communications—even when you're speaking on the phone, believe it or not.

▶ Avoid obscenity, expressions of anger toward others, or any "–ism."

▶ Present alternatives when you're asking for decisions.

▶ If you get hung up on a point, agree to disagree (at least for the moment) and move on to another issue.

▶ Pay a well-deserved compliment. If it's based on truth, it's not flattery but it is flattering. And it helps.

Spun Like Gold— All Communication Has an Angle

Communication is about subtlety and nuance. It's impressive to see a real pro in action, because they always know how to express something just so. With practice, it becomes second nature, but early in one's career it's smart to make a study of those who have attained mastery. Don't neglect to consider your own supervisor, because he or she might be better at it than you think. Your day-to-day work issues might blind you to your immediate manager's skill. An architect friend told me how she started out at her first job thinking her supervisor was a nemesis, but then she realized, in a flash, that this manager was very carefully cultivating my friend's abilities by pushing her just a little bit farther than she wanted to go. Of course, she had newfound respect for her supervisor, whom she now refers to as a master manager.

The best communicators understand that it's not what you say so much as how you say it. Your choice of words (and tone of voice) flavors your message. This flavor, which is known as spin, influences the recipient's reaction. For example, when you delegate a report-writing task to your assistant, you can tell him that the executive VP gets impatient with verbose writing (the stick approach) or you can emphasize that this honcho really notices and appreciates terse expression (a modified form of the carrot technique). Both statements might be equally true, but your choice of spin for this message makes a big difference in the impact it will have. And your decision will depend on multiple factors, including your assistant's style.

The finest spinmeisters are like great pickpockets or magicians: You don't even realize it's happening. Spin is not readily apparent, but it's very powerful. Spin isn't about the content of the message; it's about the inflection, what's being implied. Good spin does its work without making anyone aware of its presence.

Think Like a Spinner—Without Getting Dizzy

The way to develop spinning talents is by conscious practice. First, strive to notice spin in all its varieties. Advertisements are nearly too easy. It's more useful to focus on individual interaction: how people get the outcomes they desire. Try some experiments on your own. Write the same brief memo in

MATCHING TECHNOLOGY TO CONTENT

With such an embarrassment of interpersonal communication riches, it's easier than ever to embarrass yourself. Accidentally send an e-mail to the wrong person, and you can be in serious trouble. Or convene a meeting to discuss a matter that's better handled privately, and you could look like a tactless boor. Ask someone a question on the phone that requires him or her to think it over, and you might get an answer very different from what you expected. And so on. The range of communication media can seem at times like an elaborate place setting with twelve different forks and knives: Which should be used when?

The following guide provides a basic framework for matching technology to subject matter and tone. But you'll encounter exceptions from time to time, so flexibility is advised.

Telephone

When to use: For a huge range of communication, whether brief or protracted. Conversations where the human element is key—to convey warmth, anger, and so on.

When not to use: When the subject matter is very sensitive, in-person contact is often preferable, because of the heightened role of facial expression and body language. Also, if the other party tends to run off at the mouth, phone work should be restricted to times when time is not an issue.

Conference calls

When to use: Real-time, multiple-location conversations, such as resolving confusion about a project's timetable or assigned roles.

When not to use: Nearly always; unless the phone system is better than average, delays and voice dropouts too often make conference calls an irksome process. Any time strong emotions or expression will be involved. Sensitive negotiations should be handled in person.

Video conference

When to use: For discussions and negotiations involving multiple people at more than one location; especially useful when one side is arrayed against another (though not always in opposition).

When not to use: Any other situation; setting up a videoconference is a big undertaking. But in-person negotiations should be arranged for major or critical deals or decisions, unless that's impossible.

Voice mail

When to use: To let parties know you've returned their calls, but you must specify who is to take the next step. If all that's necessary is an answer to a question, voice mail is fine; messages can be left during off-hours. To make arrangements (when the other person doesn't have e-mail or doesn't check it often).

When not to use: For sensitive issues where a conversation is needed, not a mere message. Or

(continued)

issues where a paper trail is called for, such as reprimands. To offer apologies, or complex explanations for problems. Any time the communication must be extensive.

E-mail

When to use: Only with people who are "wired" and who actively check their e-mail. Fast-and-dirty ideas or messages—when both parties have their e-mail up and running, such as during normal work hours. Back-and-forth matters; brainstorming by e-mail can work well. Making arrangements for an event or meeting. Situations where you want to compose your thoughts and expressions carefully, but only if you know the other party uses e-mail in a similar manner; if not, stick with a memo or letter.

When not to use: Dealing with any issue where misinterpretation could easily happen. Sensitive issues in general. When the communication might be seen as "spam"—that is, promotion, marketing, or advertising. For long printed documents—expecting recipients to print them out is unwise. Do not e-mail anything you don't want "forwarded" to anyone else.

U.S. postal service

When to use: When you need to send official or extensive printed material and time is not extremely tight. To send catalogs or other promotional materials. To create a postmarked paper trail. (Although printed-out e-mails can sometimes suffice.)

When not to use: Tight time-critical situations. When back-and-forth discussion is desirable.

Overnight express service (including U.S. mail)

When to use: When printed material must be received the following day and/or when a package is valuable and must be traceable.

When not to use: Any time normal mail will suffice. To make an impression of urgency—this can work well or backfire just as easily.

Informal chat

When to use: To settle noncomplex, nonsensitive matters—those you're sure can be handled quickly.

When not to use: More in-depth conversations, sensitive subjects; any time backup documentation is required.

Arranged face-to-face meeting

When to use: For most work-related discussions, especially complex or extensive conversations or brainstorming sessions. If documentation is required.

When not to use: For issues or questions that could be handled by a simple phone call or e-mail. Or for matters that should be dealt with in the presence of others—as witnesses or because they're affected as well.

Formal meeting

When to use: When multiple parties need to discuss business matters. Debriefing sessions. Important announcements.

When not to use: Any other time.

several different styles, giving each version a different spin. For example, with one version you could try to motivate people about a common project, and with another suggest that there's a clash between finance and marketing that's hobbling the project. Ask someone you know (perhaps even your manager) to evaluate them. Ask her what effects she thinks the different versions would have. Do her perceptions correspond with your intentions?

Once you've started to actively think in terms of spin, your communication will become more strategically directed. It's a never-ending process, and you'll continually run across people from whom you can learn more refinements.

Different Strokes for Different Media

Knowing when and how much to communicate is fundamental, and understanding how to get your points across is essential. But it's also critical that you tailor your message to make the best use of the particular information platform you choose.

Each communication medium is better for some uses than others. With more media available than ever before, the opportunities for customizing your communication system are great, but the complexity and new challenges we face mean that there's a lot of confusion out in the work world. It wasn't long ago when you had three basic options for communicating: speak, phone, or write. Now, of course, there are dozens—a teleconference is really a medium unto itself, for example, with its own etiquette and operating instructions.

I've noticed that there's a real cutoff between the pre- and post-PC generations. There's some reluctance among older people to take technology by the horns and get the most out of it, just as there's a simple lack of awareness among younger workers that there was ever a world without e-mail. The majority of the work world doesn't yet run on e-mail; the telephone—including voice mail—is still the primary medium of choice between people at different companies. And of course, above all, there's the face-to-face conversation, which is an art form as well as a strategic craft.

Younger people in the office tend to have less understanding of the right way to communicate via old-fashioned media, just as the older cohorts can't always seem to get the hang of the newfangled equipment. But even with an ever-accelerating change of pace, there will be the need for a variety of communication forms. What matters most is to know which ones are appropriate for particular purposes, and of course how to make optimal use of the medium or media you employ.

Everybody has pet peeves when it comes to how employees should or shouldn't express themselves, and not all of my suggestions will suit you perfectly. But the following ideas stick mostly to the essential points, and are intended to help you avoid the bad habits that people at work often have or fall into.

Let's Face It—Conversations

At its best, conversation is an art form. At its best at work, it's the most powerful tool you have to curry influence. It seems that the quality of conversation is on the downswing, as a result of video games and other diversions that cut into our face-to-face communication time. But the basic principles are intact, and anyone who gets them down pat has an excellent advantage in the work world.

- ▶ Keep this in mind: Even in a work context, conversation is usually a form of mental dancing. The finest conversationalists lead so expertly that their partner believes they're actually leading.

- ▶ Keep this in mind too: Conversation can be a form of dueling, especially in a work context. Stay on your toes even as you avoid trampling on theirs.

- ▶ Always make eye contact, but don't fix your conversation partner in a bug-eyed stare. Keep it relaxed, but keep your sight focused on them.

- ▶ A little smiling goes a long way (as long as you don't appear to be smirking, of course, or flashing a politician's teeth). Smile easily, and people will enjoy speaking with you more than they do with nonsmilers.

- ▶ Personalize it. Use the other person's name, and keep "you" as a subject in any communication. The name technique is surprisingly powerful. Try to avoid the "I" trap. When people speak, "I" is often the most common word.

- ▶ Ask your partner questions; ask if she agrees with your points, or just what she thinks. Make it collaborative.

- ▶ Try to avoid, or at least cut back on, the American space-fillers, like "like," "y'know," "I mean," "well." You notice it when someone has a bad case of the filler habit, and they don't seem as with it as they should. We're so used to a certain amount of those meaningless interjections that it's a real pleasure to speak to someone who uses only words that mean something.

▶ If you have a smooth, melodious speaking voice, you're very fortunate. By all means, work it. If you don't—or especially if you have reason to think your voice is especially grating or monotonous—you might seriously consider a little voice training. If you know how to use your voice, you can get away with saying anything. Practice modulating your pitch, and speaking with a confident, calm tone, at a steady but not monotonous tempo. Practice saying the most grueling utterances you can think of (i.e., emotionally painful stuff) without losing your in-control tone. In the event of workplace psychodramas, being able to control your voice will help you control everything else—even your mood, to some degree.

▶ Avoid buzzwords, anything that you have to put in ironic quote marks. Or keep them to a minimum. It's annoying to feel that you can't escape the advertising culture even when you're talking to another person. TV show phrases are a sorry excuse for realness.

▶ Laugh at your conversation partner's jokes, and the person will love you. You'll find that the more powerful people are, the more easily everyone around them laughs at their jokes, whether or not they're even funny. When you chuckle or laugh at someone's joke, you make him or her feel important as well as amusing. Of course, it can't come off as false; it has to seem natural. And if you can take a humorous riff off theirs

MEETINGS AND SEATINGS

In essence, meetings are staged events where force of personality sometimes matters much more than force of argument. Power maneuvering is always the subtext when corporate professionals convene. Some employees know how to score points and come out ahead, while others flounder and lose ground. It's a matter of presentation.

Brushing up on your public-speaking skills always works in your favor (as does careful grooming and dressing), but some other, specific tactics are:

▶ Show up for meetings on time or early—never late. Early offers two benefits: (1) by participating in the premeeting banter, you have an influence on the tone and agenda of the meeting,

and work with it, so that you two are mentally playing . . . well, that's about as good as conversation gets. One or two interactions of that type and a true bond is formed. To attempt that and flop, though, is very uncomfortable for both participants.

▶ Do not laugh excessively at your own jokes. It comes off as extremely self-involved. But if you want the other person to be able to laugh, at least smile yourself.

and (2) it allows you to choose your location, which can make a tremendous difference.

▶ If you want to be a power player, then sit directly across from your boss—or whoever else is chairing the meeting. Obviously, this raises your profile in the leader's mind.

▶ But if you want to appear to be a right-hand person, then sit in the seat to the leader's right; that's the origin of the phrase, after all.

▶ If the head player is a lefty, then sit on that side of her, because that's the side from which she naturally tends to gather information.

▶ If it's a low profile you're after, then sitting three seats or so down from your boss will make it hard for her to focus on you.

▶ Always take notes, or have a pad and pen at the ready. Not being prepared to record what's discussed or decided can be seen as a lack of diligence, or even arrogance.

▶ If you need to have an extensive conversation, try to do so somewhere comfortable rather than in a corridor. Also, don't do it where there will inevitably be interruptions, even if they're minor, such as people passing by and nodding hello. Make the other person feel as if he or she is your single priority while you converse.

▶ Do not whisper. Whispering attracts attention. The more people whisper, the closer others listen. Any attempt to speak especially quietly makes everyone's ears perk up, in the assumption that you're discussing them. This applies to phone communication too.

▶ Watch your body language. Don't stand with crossed arms unless you want to project the image of a stubborn opponent. Generally, it means a conversation is going well when the two participants' postures mirror each other.

▶ If you think you misheard the other person or vice versa, make sure to clarify whatever was said. That can make all the difference; it's amazing how consequential a single misheard syllable can be.

Get Them to Talk Straight with You

Getting other people to be straightforward with you can be a conversational challenge. Some workers believe they need to protect their turf, or they're trying to cover up their own insecurities or even incompetence, and so you'll never get a direct reply. If you're having trouble getting a straight answer, try these tactics:

▶ Come right out and tell them you want a direct reply. "OK, I can take it: What do we have to do to make the business plan acceptable to investors? Just give it to me straight."

▶ Keep on asking. Rephrase the same question a few times, and their resistance might succumb to attrition. If not, find another angle on the question: "Is there too little competitor research?" "Do you think we went overboard on market analysis and too light on the numbers?" "Do you think there's a better opportunity in that area?"

- ▶ Tell them you value their intelligence and insight and judgment—and taste in restaurants, if that will help. Don't come off as insincere, but don't be hesitant to give them a stake. "I know there's something that could be improved in the plan, but I don't have the experience to pick it out. But I know that you have helped launch about seven companies now, or you at least played key strategic roles. So I figured you'd be the best manager in the company to ask."

- ▶ Ask if there's a problem that's preventing them from answering. "I can't help but wonder whether this is a business that you were planning on trying out. Is that the case?" This is a somewhat confrontational device, so it should be employed only when all else fails.

- ▶ The next step is to suggest that a higher-up will have to be involved. An alternative is to say, "Let's figure this out together, rather than waiting till the VPs decide they have to investigate." That tack can knock down a lot of walls.

Dials—Phone Style

Few professionals get very far if they don't have strong phone skills. Most of your interactions with people outside your immediate company (or even your department) are phone-mediated, so you'd better know how to make it work for you.

Most of the suggestions for face-to-face conversations apply to phone work as well, even the part about smiling. It comes through in your voice. It's always a pleasure to speak with someone who's a true phone maestro. Here too having an appealing voice is a huge boon. If you tend to be nasal, on the other hand, the phone amplifies that effect.

► Watch out for bad speech habits. If you mumble, speak too rapidly, speak too softly, whine, or anything else that makes it hard for people to pick out your words, that will make phone conversations with you highly irritating. Ask your friends about your phone manner, about whether it could use some improvement, and if so, how.

► If you spend a lot of time on the phone at work, definitely get a headset. If your company won't spring for it, buy it yourself. You can find some that work just fine at Radio Shack for less than $50. The quality-of-life and ease-of-work gains are significant, such as no more neck cricks, freed-up hands, and a more natural speaking tone.

► If you're multitasking (opening your mail, say, or sorting papers), don't think your phone partner doesn't hear it. Some people can't stand that attention split; they'd prefer sixty seconds of your pure attention than five minutes of your half-there focus. And they have a point.

► It's considerate to open a conversation by asking whether this is a good time for the person to talk for a few minutes. Just because they picked up the phone doesn't mean they really can speak comfortably; perhaps they were just expecting a different call.

▶ If you have time constraints, make that known at the outset of the call. "I have twenty minutes before my next meeting, and I wanted to discuss those three points. I hope we can reach closure on at least two of them before I need to go. How does that sound?" And stick to your schedule, especially if the person is someone with whom you'll be speaking on a regular basis. When you have an agenda, make sure to proceed through the points. If one is sticking you both up, then go on to the next and double back at the end if you have the time.

Voice-Mail Training

Sure, this is a part of phone work, but it's also a medium unto itself. With all the focus on e-mail, a lot of people are neglecting this extremely practical form of communication—but that's because they don't know all the fine points. These suggestions will help you avoid important pitfalls and show you how to take voice mail to the next level.

▶ Make your messages brief, succinct, and coherent. Don't speak too quickly; voice mail loses some sonic accuracy. Don't ramble—no one wants to hear your stream-of-consciousness gibberish in a phone message, not even your best friend. Messages should be no longer than they need to be.

way to go! I had an employee who consistently left me voice mails at eleven P.M. to update me about whatever he'd finished up that evening; frequently that would help me out the next morning, so he wasn't just asking for gold stars. He kept the messages brief—thirty seconds, tops. When it came time for raises, he got the highest in the company. (It wasn't just the messages, by the way; he also accomplished a lot of work between 9:30 and 6:30!)

▶ Always leave your phone number. Someone could be calling in for their messages and not have your number with them.

▶ Never return or send an internal voice mail when you're angry. Anything you say is there for good; it can't be retracted, but it can be forwarded within the company. Adopt an approach similar to the twenty-four-hour rule described earlier in the chapter.

▶ Never return or leave a voice mail when you're drunk. The receiving party will hear it in your voice, and it is considered ultra-bad form in a work-related context. (It's not so sharp in civilian life either.)

▶ Don't leave messages when you're lying down; your voice will sound constricted and your attitude of repose will translate into an unbusinesslike tone.

▶ Always return phone calls within twenty-four hours. Even if you have thirty messages, anyone can find the time—just do it late at night to the callers' work numbers, and at least you'll have replied.

▶ Often, the best way to convey information is to leave a voice mail when the other person isn't there, either before or after work hours. A full conversation would be a mutual waste of time, but they needed reassurance about something or some straightforward communication. This method is ideal.

▶ Use the time stamp function to your benefit. When you leave a voice mail message for your boss at eleven P.M., that demonstrates your zeal to get a project finished (or your utter lack of time-management abilities). On the flip side, if you're leaving voice mail for your employees at two A.M. on a Saturday, you're letting them know that you don't have much of a life.

wrong turn! I had another employee who was a diligent worker but had an extremely annoying habit of calling my machine and leaving interminable messages about his schedule. He always seemed to remember on a weekend or a day off that he wanted to take an additional day off as a vacation day or whatever. He was very impulsive, and he needed to let me know at that very minute what he was thinking. I found myself replying abruptly, in annoyance at the duration of his messages rather than his request, and telling him "No, you cannot have that day off." And then I would have to call him back and retract that. But it's indicative of how incredibly annoying it can be when someone leaves you eight-minute messages.

▶ It's a good idea to change your message on a daily basis. Many people find voice mail too impersonal. By maintaining a topical message, you humanize the medium a little.

► Don't leave a message if you're not completely sure you're reached the right extension. Some very embarrassing situations can ensue if you slip up and misdial. In general, it's best to not impart sensitive information by voice mail unless you have no choice.

Write On—Memos, Letters, Etc.

Writing isn't a lost art, but good writing is hard to come by in the corporate world. Those who know how to do it right have a large advantage in composing effective letters, memos, reports, and even brief notes. It's easy to detect the difference between a skilled writer and someone who never really learned those skills.

In recent years, in fact, English professors have been making good money teaching business executives writing skills. It's still more important to be a charismatic speaker if you want to move forward in business, but quality writing is impressive and it does get noticed.

A lot of people are writing more than they used to, even if most of the pieces are short, as a result of e-mail. Which is no doubt a good thing, for as long as it lasts; there are already voice-activated e-mail and Web surfing programs available.

Anyone who wants to hone their writing skills can find plenty of resources through bookstores, software marts, continuing ed courses, executive training workshops, and so on. But the first place to start is probably with the old perennial *The Elements of Style*, by Strunk and White.

A few basic points about business writing:

▶   To put something in writing makes it official, so choose carefully what you decide to write up. (E-mails are just as official, by the way; they qualify as part of the paper trail, even though they seem less permanent than paper letters. And they can be retrieved easily enough from the company's archival data.) When something is put into official form, say a written warning to an employee who's underperforming, it carries more psychic weight than an e-mail or handwritten note. Managers are very careful in how they phrase employee performance reviews, for example, because companies can be exposed to litigation if a document is poorly composed. Anything that's put into writing is ammo for the recipient to use if the going gets ugly, so verbal methods usually come first.

▶   On the other hand, a letter on company stationery has dignity; it seems to ennoble the message. You would want a letter of recommendation to be presented in that format. And when you send a letter like that thanking a supplier, you convey a deeper level of appreciation than you would with an e-mail.

▶   When something is written, it's tangible; everyone now knows how you chose to represent the minutes of the all-company meeting. Perhaps your departmental bias is evident; or perhaps your personal sense of humor is displayed, and it clicks well enough so you come to be considered the company scribe, which leads to a promotion within six months to VP of communications. For better or worse, there it is, for all to see and to reread as many times as they care to.

▶ Because of this, the spin factor must be subtle; not so blatant that anyone can see the effort to influence opinion or outcome.

▶ Written documents should be impeccable—no spelling errors; perfectly formatted; no White-Out smudges. The word processor's spellcheck function isn't an adequate safeguard; you might have included entirely wrong words that are spelled correctly. Every document must be proofread by at least one person who's practiced in that craft.

▶ Clarity is paramount in all business writing. Especially in the case of official documents, precision comes before style. Also, without any nonverbal cues, the words themselves must convey the tone, the full meaning. (Emoticons are not permissible.)

▶ Generally, it's possible to go back over a draft and find many places where words can be removed at no loss to the meaning; all such words should be yanked if you're trying to make the writing as elegant as possible.

▶ Factor in plenty of time to write something special. It's obvious when a piece is a last-minute rush job.

No matter how professionally advanced you become, clear and careful writing will remain invaluable.

E-Mail—Extra Vigilance Required

In many quarters, e-mail has taken the world by storm. At countless companies, the majority of interpersonal communications are now sent electronically. It's reduced the development time in some industries, including publishing, graphic design, and engineering. Entire departments have scaled back employee rolls because of the productivity the Net offers. Purchasing departments, for example, now routinely communicate on-line with all their suppliers; they make sure to use a secure line, of course.

E-mail is a terrific medium, and one that's made a lot of workers more efficient. Perhaps the best use of e-mail is to alleviate confusion without wasting time. By soliciting answers to straightforward questions via e-mail, you avoid the conversations that are likely when you ask the same questions on the telephone or face-to-face—the "since you're here" phenomenon. E-mail also eliminates most of the time wasting and irritation of phone tag.

Or perhaps you're trying to clarify an issue with another worker that references a departmentwide memo; instead of hunting down the document, photocopying it to attach to your memo, you can just copy and paste the relevant sections into your e-mail. Deploying e-mail can save you hundreds of hours a year that you would have had to expend in the old days. (The problem with such a time-saver is that then you're expected to do that much more work, and then some.)

Another great application is sending (by secure connection, of course) large documents back and forth to distant geographical locations—and distant means any locale outside of bicycle messenger range. Instead of overnighting a report finished at the eleventh and a half hour, you just e-mail it to the five recipients as a PDF file, and they print out the equivalent of a publication-quality brochure on their respective laser machines. An author I know was telling me recently how his latest book would have taken at least two weeks longer to write were it not for e-mail. Changes are highlighted, so the parties know who wrote what, or comments can be imbedded in the text. (The role of sophisticated word processing and desktop-publishing software should also be celebrated.)

But e-mail is treacherous as well. I know of more than a dozen stories in which people actually lost their jobs because they failed to realize that e-mail documents might be held and used against you. I have personally lost friends over e-mail "forwards."

So, here are some essential tips to bear in mind when using e-mail. Most of them apply to nonnetworked memo-writing as well.

Don't write anything that you wouldn't put into an old-fashioned memo. It's that paper trail factor. Even after an e-mail is deleted, your company's systems operator can easily retrieve it. At this point in time, a majority of large American companies monitor their employees' e-mail correspondence. Whether or not you think that's a violation of privacy (the truth is, there is no such thing as privacy when you work for a corporation), you must be extremely vigilant never to put into writing anything that could come back to haunt you.

Watch your tone. In person, your tone of voice conveys as much as your words do. If you ask your boss whether a scheduled client meeting is really necessary, you can show that you're deferring to their judgment even as you call a matter into question. Try doing that by e-mail, though, and it'll sound like rank insubordination. If you can't resist occasionally injecting some levity into an e-mail that could be misconstrued, then add a parenthetical "just kidding."

Be terse, but not curt. I've seen two extremes. One is blabber. You ask a simple question or send a brief greeting, and they reply with a rambling, too-personal essay on what's happening in their jobs and their lives. Just because it's easy to type quickly doesn't mean you should go on at length. These aren't letters to your aunt Sally; they're business communications. Don't spill your guts, or waste the other person's time.

The other extreme is to overcompress your message. E-mails aren't haiku. You're allowed more than seventeen syllables, and there's no call for evocative or impressionistic writing. If you're a frustrated poet, express that somewhere else. Also, e-mails don't need to read like telegrams from old movies. Full sentences are fine. Of course, one-word replies are okay too at times. If so, however, always include the sender's question in your response. To illustrate: I once sent an e-mail to an executive in which I posed a series of three questions. When I received his reply, three days later, it read just this: "The answers to your questions are, respectively: $60,000. Yes. New Jersey." I didn't remember exactly what he was responding to, since I'd sent off a few dozen e-mails in the interim. So I had to dig up my e-mail from the "sent" folder. So his e-mail caused me hassle rather than convenience. All he had to do was to simply include my questions in his note.

Use standard spelling and syntax. Just because e-mail makes it easy to send off speedy replies doesn't mean you should refer to yourself as "i." Or that you're replying to someone known as "u"! It creates a terrible impression whenever I receive messages including spellings like gonna or such accepted cyber-abbreviations as IMHO (that's "in my humble opinion," in case you've been hiding under a rock). Also, avoid tired,

ELEMENTS OF COMMUNICATION

Whether it's a phone message, presentation, meeting, memo, or conversation, some basic advice applies across the board:

▶ *Prepare.* Practice what you have to say, draw up outlines, do a couple of drafts, order your slides carefully. Make sure the final product is a polished version, not a rough draft. I know an executive who reads every one of his speeches out loud to an audience—Gherkin and Puzzle (his cat and dog, respectively).

▶ *Be as brief as possible.* This is a fundamental law of politeness. Even ten extra seconds on a voice mail is enough to be truly annoying when the recipient is operating in high-caffeine mode. Of course, when a presentation is involved, you need to pace the material so people have time to assimilate it.

▶ *Use the medium's tools of clarity.* In an e-mail, make the "subject" line meaningful. In writing, construct the piece with short, logically

pseudo-hip usages such as calling everything "stuff" or claiming to be "pumped." That kind of thing is about as original as wearing a baseball cap.

Save important e-mails. Treat substantive e-mail messages the same as you would written documents—file them. Do not just leave them in your in e-mail in-box; reserve the in-box

ordered paragraphs. In presentations, frame each slide and don't overcrowd them with material. In voice messages, speak (fairly) slowly and (very) clearly.

▶ *Make it interesting.* If you're speaking, modulate your voice. If you're writing, try to make the language interesting rather than business-sterile.

▶ *Solicit questions or answers.* Whether or not it goes without saying, don't let it go without saying: "If you have any questions or feedback, please let me know."

▶ *Make it actionable.* Every communication should include a clear notice of what you desire or require of the recipient or the audience, and how they can most easily accomplish this.

▶ *Offer a good wrap-up.* Your summary should be proportionate to the medium. In an e-mail, it might be merely a closer phrase: "Hope you have time to meet with her." For a presentation, the wrap-up might be the final four slides, each of which contains a bulleted list of the four parts of your program.

exclusively for messages that have yet to be answered. Save important messages into your hard drive in project- or correspondent-specific folders, and give each e-mail a descriptive name and date.

Proofread. Carefully reread every note, however brief, before you hit "send." This gives you another shot at judging whether the material is appropriate, plus you'll presumably catch some typos, which are simply bad form. This is especially important with e-mail messages, or any documents, generated with the use of voice recognition software. A recent newspaper article recounted a story where an executive dictated a memo, which he then sent to several people, in which he'd said they should all gather en masse to meet each other and discuss the project. His VR software, however, isn't up on its French, and so it transliterated the phrase as "enemas." One of the recipients sent back a tongue-in-cheek comment to the effect that it seems like a rather extreme way to get to know each other.

Proofread everything that has your name at the top. If you're not a great speller, then be certain to spellcheck every note more than a sentence long. And spellcheck itself isn't enough on an important letter or document. Have someone else proof your work as well.

Don't jump rank. E-mail can be an especially direct mode of communication, but that doesn't mean it's okay to leapfrog over your manager and her manager to address an issue directly with the sales VP. (If you're willing to take that risk, though, and have reason to believe it will work, then more power to you.)

Do not try to intimidate people through your use of the "cc" line. And nothing is more inappropriate than copying people who shouldn't be copied.

Never use a corporate e-mail address or server for personal use—especially not for job hunting.

Double check that the e-mail is going to the right person. Once you start putting in the letters, someone elses name may come up. Double-check to be sure you are sending to the right person.

Across a Crowded Room—Presentations

Making group presentations is an extremely powerful form of self-promotion, if you can pull it off smoothly. For example, if you have an innovative idea to add to a marketing program, presenting it before a group gives you far more ownership than a memo or even a citation from your manager at the staff meeting. When you present before a group, you become a teacher; everyone gets to experience you in an elevated role. It's a great opportunity, so grab the chance if it comes your way, or suggest it to your manager whenever there's some justification.

There are two dimensions to the challenge of work-related presentations: (1) public speaking, and (2) preparing materials to be effective in this context. The first component is more important by far. For preparing materials, at least there are software programs that make the task logical and straightforward; no such technological leg-up exists to help you get over the jitters associated with speaking before a group. In fact, the main points about preparing demonstration materials can be summed up quite specifically, as follows:

▶ Set everything up ahead of time, and run through the presentation to be sure the materials are in the right order and condition. If you're using your laptop to make a presentation for a small group, make sure the Quicktime (or other presentation package) slides are all viewable. Adjust the apparatus in the meeting room to maximize image size and avoiding obstruction by meeting members.

- ▶ If you'll be using a pointer with the audiovisual device, learn how to use it before the meeting begins.

- ▶ Each slide should present a bite-size amount of information, not a smorgasbord. Make sure all the text is legible, with space between the lines of text. Make sure there's an ample border on each slide.

- ▶ Number the slides in an outline framework to make it easier for participants to "place" the material.

- ▶ Go light on the cutesy. It's better to reserve the humor for your narration.

The public-speaking phobia can't be addressed with a series of bullets. If such situations are a problem for you, you owe it to yourself to work on this. Obviously, if presentations are an ongoing part of your job, you must deal with it or else you'll hate this part of your work and will fail to execute it as well as you can. Reading books won't help most people very much. It's an experience-based fear, and calls for an experience-based solution. Just hoping that you'll gradually become less nervous over the years is a bad approach. The way to go is by joining Toastmasters or signing up for some other training program. Most companies are willing to foot the bill for such workshops because they make employees more effective.

way to go! Thomas, a brilliant, mid-level manager in a large corporation, came up with great innovative ideas on a regular basis. He could write about them quite well, but when it came time to pitch them in person to the rest of his department or to outside colleagues, he clammed up. He had such a fear of speaking that he continually gave away his own presentations, letting someone else pinch hit for him. By staying mute, he was remaining invisible. He was giving away his opportunity for advancement by not describing his ideas himself. After seeing more than a couple of colleagues advance after presenting his ideas, Thomas sought the help of a professional speaking coach, spent time rehearsing his next presentation with a trusted coworker, and was able to describe a major project to his board of directors—in his own very effective voice.

Whether or not nervousness is a big factor for you, it's always smart to practice your presentation. If you have a colleague or family member willing to critique it, that's great. If not, do so out loud anyway; try taping it and then listen to what it sounds like.

And during the presentation, keep these points in mind:

▶ Look at your audience, not the screen. Fasten on one or two people in the audience who aren't sitting adjacent to each other; use them as anchor points but make some eye contact with as many others as you can. Spend very little time turned away from the audience, and never turn your back to them.

▶ Speak at a measured pace. The tendency is to rush through the script, but you need to speak a little more slowly than in normal conversation. Again, build in a little white space. If people are taking notes, pause a bit after key points, and repeat them.

▸ Smile. Too often, presentations are grim or mono-tonous, so liven them up by a moderate amount of banter, and vary your voice patterns.

▸ Always leave some room at the end for questions. Often, it takes a bit of prodding to get the audience to start asking. This phase is an excellent opportunity to establish your "expert status."

6

Juggling on the Job: Organization and Competence

IF YOU WANT TO SUCCEED AND PROSPER on the job, you have to stay on top of your workload. That would seem to go without saying, but sad to say, it needs to be explicitly stated. Sheer brilliance alone isn't enough. A good attitude is not sufficient. And while I believe in it and have gone to great lengths to encourage it elsewhere in this book, being the most political animal in the office is not enough to rely on either.

Whoever you are, whatever you do, and however you play the game, there's one common essential ingredient for success: Handle your job effectively. And what this comes down to is knowing how to manage your time, organize your workspace, and deal with information on the job. That's what this chapter is about.

There are three essential steps to effective job performance:

1. Be crystal clear on which part of your responsibilities matters the most. The way most jobs are designed, it's not possible to do absolutely everything included in the job description. So it's crucial that you know what's really expected and wanted of you.

Generally, this boils down to one fundamental thing (such as managing a department, generating creative ad ideas, or investing the company's profits), but nearly always the job also includes one or two lesser activities that are still vital. You must not overlook these. When I speak to employees who have been laid off, some are indignant because they claim they did their basic job so well. Usually, they haven't grasped the whole story. For example, let's say you work in a firm's information management division (i.e., you're a computer techie). It's a given that you're competent at troubleshooting the network and its individual PCs. But at some companies, it's nearly as important that you can instruct the nontechnical people in how to use the equipment. Fixing the machines might be two-thirds of your job, but that other third matters a lot.

2. Make sure you have adequate resources. Just because you're assigned a task or project doesn't mean you've been given sufficient backup. When there's a problem, it usually falls into one (or more) of these categories:

- ▶ Not enough time has been allotted for a given project.
- ▶ You don't have the human resource backup you need

—there's no one to whom you can delegate the grunt
work, for example.

▶ You're not being included in the necessary information
loops.

▶ You haven't been provided sufficient materials, such as
a folder of relevant memos written by other workers.

In any of these cases, it's up to you to raise the flag and
wave it around. Ask for assistance. Don't worry about what
your supervisor will think of your request. Believe me, he'll
ultimately be a lot better off if you hassle him up front than
disappoint him in the stretch. Besides, he might have merely
miscalculated or forgotten something, such as the fact that the
mailroom is short-staffed over the summer, so no one is available to do your photocopying.

Always ask for what you need. Don't try to be a superhero
or a martyr.

3. Stay organized. This is the real meat and potatoes of
being an effective professional. With very few exceptions, the
people I know who have gone far in the work world are very
well organized. This doesn't mean being a neat freak. The big
successes in the world certainly aren't any tidier than most
people are, but they are in control of their resources. They
understand how to apportion their mental energy, how to
manage their time so they accomplish the things that matter
most to them, how to make the best use of whatever space
they work and live in, and how to gather and structure the
information they need.

If you can succeed at managing what I call the three primary resources—time, space, and information—then there's

way to go!　　I knew Andrea was the top sales rep at the company where she worked, but I couldn't figure out why she wasn't getting better territories to ply over time. At year end, of course, she received the hefty bonuses she'd earned, but the company wasn't advancing her—not only were they neglecting to improve her turf, but she hadn't received any of the other forms of recognition, such as a management title. I'd grill her about this, but it wasn't until I'd known her for a couple of years that she conceded she was "not the most reliable person in the world when it comes to doing the paperwork." In other words, she occasionally neglected to completely fill out all the sales order documentation, or she made mistakes in her haste to get it over with. Obviously, she hated this part of her job: "I live to sell, not to fiddle around with scraps of paper." But her lackadaisical attitude toward the administrative side of things created problems for the company's accounting and shipping departments. I read her the riot act about this, and to my amazement she actually changed her ways. (People usually resist good advice for a long time.) Andrea became extremely meticulous and prompt about her paperwork, partly because I'd virtually guaranteed her that she'd reap tangible benefits from doing so. Also, Andrea was tired of the stress that came from perpetually avoiding the paperwork; so it was a relief for her to turn this corner. Within a year, her situation at the company had improved drastically, and the very next Christmas she was offered the position of regional manager—and in this case the company was willing to adjust the position's duties so Andrea could still spend most of her time doing sales.

no reason you should run into any major difficulties accomplishing your workload. Staying organized is the key to doing an above-average job. (And don't forget that getting organized isn't as hard as remaining that way.) In fact, being organized will put you in the lucky minority, because this is one area where people struggle horribly—much more than they should have to. The advice that fills the rest of this chapter is likely to save you a lot of aggravation and perhaps even years of bumbling. It will allow you to focus on what counts the most—cultivating workplace contacts and making smart political moves.

It's About Time . . .

Time-management problems seem to be some sort of an epidemic and national preoccupation. There are racks of books offering advice on the subject, from the mundane to the spiritual. And it's big business for personal consultants and coaches too. Everybody seems to be on edge about whether they have enough time to do all they need to do, especially at work. It's among the top five problems I hear about from radio callers.

To a degree, this time bind is the result of companies driving their people at 125 percent of capacity. To get by, most middle-class families definitely need two salaries. And downsizing turned up the heat for a lot of employees. But I think these factors are somewhat exaggerated. In most office environments, working conditions aren't that severe. (And if yours are, this is a good time to seek more reasonable climes.)

Nearly all time problems are self-created. In general, they stem from three common tendencies: procrastination, work for work's sake, or inability to make decisions. In fact, many

TIME-SAVERS

I've read and heard thousands of tips on how to shave off a few minutes here and there from everyday work tasks. The following list comprises a selection of the ones that really work—with a few caveats that lists of this sort don't generally include.

▶ Use a cell phone. They're great for making productive use of otherwise dead time. When an architectural firm owner I know had jury duty, he stayed on top of things with his wireless. Instead of spending three hours a night at his company after jury duty, he got by with an hour every other day. Of course, don't use the phone from locations where reception is terrible. The point is to be more efficient, not to annoy people.

▶ Read the paper before work, not at the job. This should be obvious, but huge numbers of people make this error.

▶ Don't take a half hour to get cooking once you get to work; give yourself five minutes.

▶ Clear your desk at the end of the day. Just leave out the one item you want to launch into the next morning.

▶ Keep a clock in your work space. A clock is more adamant about time passing—you can't as easily ignore a clock as you can a watch. A clock is a useful way to pace yourself too.

▶ Instead of listening to your voice mails when

you get to work, get some other things done first to give your day momentum. (Obviously, at some jobs this isn't an option.)

▶ Return your nonurgent voice mails after work hours. Even if you do so after the nightly news, at 11:30, that's fine. No one cares when a message is sent, as long as they get their response. When people claim they "didn't have a chance" to return a phone call, I think—or ask—"What are you saying?" Everyone can return their phone calls, just not necessarily during business hours. The after-hour approach is perfect for calls that require only a confirmation or quick answer; leaving a message is far better than getting sidetracked in an unnecessary conversation.

▶ Keep lunch brief, but make sure to give yourself a substantial break some time during the day. Taking a brisk walk is just as important as eating. Do make sure to load up on enough calories to keep you going for the whole day, but don't overeat so that you get hit with the mid-afternoon crash every day. No one who wants to be efficient takes a whole hour for lunch—half an hour is generally plenty.

▶ If you're a caffeine user, consider keeping your coffee or tea apparatus at your desk. Just don't let your cubicle turn into an informal cafe.

▶ Put in your extra hours before regular work hours, not after. It's far easier to get things done before you've expended a whole workday's worth

(continued)

of energy, and you're less likely to be distracted. (Send off a few e-mails or voice mails to your supervisor and other higher-level managers while you're at it, so your diligence is duly noted.)

▶ If you have an office, work the closed-door option. Keep it shut for a couple of hours a day, and use that time to tear through concentration-intensive tasks or handle tricky phone work. Make sure your supervisor knows this is intensive work time, not kickback. When others realize that you're not available 100 percent of the day, they won't just frivolously wander over to your office.

▶ If you can use music headphones at your company, try putting on some background-type music or environmental sounds at a low volume for part of the day. When you're wearing phones, others are less likely to interrupt you.

▶ Avoid business lunches as much as possible. They're time killers. And when you do go, don't have any alcohol, unless you're willing to blow off the rest of the day. (Of course, the occasional lunch is politically necessary, but tightly limit those, and make each one count.)

▶ When appropriate, answer memos or letters by writing your reply directly on the document and making a copy for your records. But be very sensitive to the question of appropriateness. It's usually off base to apply this technique on notes from anyone higher up the ladder than you. Some supervisors will accept this method (because it's in their own best interest), but make sure to get permission before trying it. The scrawled comment technique tends to remind people of teachers' comments on papers, so be especially alert to your tone. Make sure you write very clearly.

▶ When you need to brainstorm or collaborate with another worker or two, do it with quick conversations at one of your cubicles rather than formal meetings or elaborate memos. Write a quick note to confirm any decisions to prevent claims of ignorance or miscommunication afterwards.

▶ Act upon every piece of mail or other incoming material as soon as it's received; toss it, delegate the matter and pass it on, write a quick response, file it, or place it in the "on-deck circle" to be dealt with at a definite time. Nothing should be left up in the air.

▶ Maintain a samurai attitude about personal phone calls. The less personal stuff you deal with on the job, the more you'll be able to finish your work in a timely manner and leave.

▶ Also, maintain that attitude with respect to meetings. At a meeting scheduled to last forty minutes, for example, start to wrap it up at the thirty-six-minute mark. Take your own schedule seriously and you make other people do the same. But be sensible. If you're dealing with a tremendously important ally, don't abruptly curtail a discussion unless you have no choice. If you're not the one in charge of an important meeting, don't schedule later events too tightly.

time-challenged workers are bedeviled by more than one of these traits.

Procrastination. Fortunately, I'm not personally afflicted by this tendency, but I can see it's a serious problem for many employees. Once you fall behind, it's not easy to catch up. Plus, your reputation suffers, as well as your self-esteem. So if that's your problem, I recommend you do anything and everything it takes to correct it. Too many bright, talented, sometimes gifted people impede themselves by procrastinating. I discuss this issue at length a little farther down.

Working for Work's Sake. This is perhaps an even bigger problem than procrastination. It seems that a lot of employees try to make up for what's missing in their outside lives by putting in ridiculous amounts of time and energy at their jobs. When I speak to people who are obviously shot from overworking at someone else's firm, I often tell them, "Look, no job is that hard. What's the real problem here?" Most of them will acknowledge that it's not just the workloads, but they can't put their finger on what's driving them. In other words, they're working for the sake of working.

In some cases, people work harder than they really need to or have to because it makes them feel and look important. Take Sharon, a small business acquaintance of mine. Whenever I speak with her, she complains about faxing to suppliers at six A.M. and working through to eleven P.M., doing "God knows what paperwork." To manage her $20 million company, Sharon is constantly sending off faxes and e-mails, and calling suppliers and customers. The business seems to be a fairly simple one, and Sharon seems well organized, but she just needs to be in motion all the time. It gives her a sense of self. Meanwhile, this psychological need of hers takes time away from any personal life.

Some tireless workers are running from terrible problems in their personal lives. One perfect example I've encountered was Martha, a recently married thirty-two-year-old executive at my first Fortune 500 employer who started working there about the same time I did. Martha would work till eight or nine every night, without fail, even though the rest of the company was out the door by five-thirty or six. Her job didn't seem any more complicated than anyone else's, but she was the lone late-nighter. In fact, I would feel guilty leaving her behind to work away for several hours more. I had no idea what she did during those hours—except that she was always loaded with paperwork. Martha seemed to revel in the feel of paper. Three years after joining the company, Martha announced that she and her architect husband were getting divorced. Apparently, as Martha shuffled her papers long into the night, he was whiling away his time having an affair.

Inability to Make Decisions. Obviously, working for work's sake is a self-destructive tendency. And chronic waffling is just as bad. This is a characteristic I come across all the time in my career—candidates can't decide whether to take a job, or which is the better between two options, and clients can't choose from among the applicant pool. In some cases, we could have hired and trained someone, seen whether they could handle the job, and fired them if it didn't work out in the time it took a client to make a decision. And during that whole period, this client had an open slot, with work piling up or all the other workers scrambling to fill the hole.

Learn to make decisions. Sitting on the fence does no one any good. It amazes me how people torment themselves, weighing the pros and the cons, when they can't know whether a decision is sound till after they make it! Most of the time, decisions are a matter of luck anyway. It's a fifty-fifty proposition. The best thing you can do is trust your gut and make the decision so you can get on with it.

What a time-management program will comprise. Many employees have no idea where to begin in establishing a functional time-management program. So here are the basic components of time management:

▶ Know how long it actually takes you to get things done, and use that knowledge to schedule your time realistically. Successful professionals don't necessarily accomplish tasks more quickly than strugglers do, but they're sensible about how much time to allocate.

▶ Underpromise and overdeliver; never overpromise. It's far better to deliver ahead of schedule.

▶ Schedule backward. Start with the end date, and then slot in what needs to be done the day before, and then move backward along the time line, making sure that each day's appointed workload is reasonable. There are a lot of advantages to this method. One is that as you plan, you're starting from a place of psychological strength—the finish line.

▶ Stick to your schedule. In other words, don't allow

yourself to be distracted. You need to be able to count on yourself. As I tell employees: Think of deadlines as the departure date on a nonrefundable plane ticket. You miss the deadline; you blow the ticket—and the vacation. When crisis interferes, make realistic schedule adjustments on the fly.

► Always keep people informed about how a project is progressing, whether it's ahead of schedule, right on time, or running behind. When you see that a significant delay is inevitable, inform the other parties that are involved or might be affected. Perhaps you'll need to call for reinforcements, or maybe it only means everyone will adjust their time expectations.

► Budget in some buffer—or mistake recovery—time. Make sure you have a clear set of damage control procedures so you can handle any contingency.

► Take care of the top priorities first; don't delude yourself that crossing off one item from the checklist is as good as crossing off another.

► Take full responsibility for your own time allocation. Don't blame outside forces or other people—that only confuses matters and introduces mental noise.

► If you slip up, timewise (and virtually everybody does occasionally), admit the error, remedy the situation if you can, and carry on. Don't let one problem knock over all the other pins, or shake you up.

► Apply triage. If you're juggling three projects, and you see they're not all going to get finished on time, make sure it's the one with the lowest priority that suffers, not the highest.

▶ Use lists, but don't turn them into an end in themselves. You shouldn't be spending half an hour every morning working on your to-do list. Everyone has his or her own method; many people maintain separate lists for work and outside life. The only element that's universal is a calendar, which should provide the foundation for all your daily lists. Never accidentally miss an appointment; it's simply unnecessary if you have a functional system in place.

Top Priority Is More Than a Buzz Phrase

Even more important than adopting (and adapting) a time-management program that suits your personality and interests

---

WORK SMARTER, NOT LONGER

The problem with becoming more efficient in today's work world is that many companies will try to penalize you for it. If you can shave 20 percent off the time it takes you to manage your workload, then you should gain most if not all of that time for yourself. (I'm assuming you, like most people, already work a lot more than forty hours a week.)

What usually happens, though, is that your manager will take advantage of your strides. She'll use your efficiency gains as an excuse to pile more work on your tray, so you still don't get out of the office before seven P.M. If you're a young and

is the ability to stick with it. A time-management program is like an exercise regimen or diet in this regard. You need to make the habits second nature, and to make sure not to slack off when it's convenient to do so. (Be extra vigilant when you return from vacation, for instance.)

Most people make lists—it seems like some type of human instinct. Making lists is a powerful technique for structuring your time and tasks. There's no single best method for list construction. Some people do just fine with a calendar and a daily to-do list, for which they assemble the items from memory. Other people need to keep elaborate sublists, perhaps because their interests are so wide-ranging and complicated (or perhaps because they're retentive). Whatever system you

hungry grad at your first job, then you might not mind being exploited, because you'll be learning so much that's new. But if you're an adult with a home life, you simply do not owe all your output as a human to the company. You should refuse to accept such "expanded responsibilities" unless the company provides an expanded paycheck. And if your highest priority is increasing personal time, then refuse to take on the extra tasks altogether— or if you have no choice, seek other employment.

In the recessionary late 1980s and early 1990s, you might have been too nervous to object, but these days workers actually have some leverage.

come up with, it should ensure that nothing important ever falls through the cracks—for example, you never forget about a personal engagement or neglect to file a particular document on time. The other imperative is that your system clarifies priorities. Perhaps you keep a rotating calendar/list on your home computer, and print out a day's worth every morning; you could sort different activities by color, for example, or signify higher priorities with a larger typeface. But it's crucial that you have some sort of cue—a visual one if you're a list keeper, a cognitive one if you just proceed from memory.

But building in a hierarchy of priorities is just half the battle. The other half—and three-quarters might be more accurate—is adhering to that recognition. This is a mental game; no one can establish an "executive function" for you. Just because you've made it through life this far as an undisciplined sort of person, if that's the case, doesn't mean (1) that you're going to continue to get by for much longer without such abilities, and (2) that it's too late to acquire some discipline at this stage in your career.

I've seen remarkable transformations occur in people from whom I least expected it. In fact, I've seen discipline kick in at unexpected times. An architectural engineer I knew was basically getting by with a minimum of fuss, just doing what came easily to him. But one year his firm was hired to oversee the redesign of a dilapidated riverfront section in St. Louis. For some reason, this project sparked an intense interest, and he brought a sensational amount of focus and creativity to the job, especially because no one suspected he really cared much for his profession. Apparently, he had a sentimental attachment to that city, which contributed to his sudden and keen activation. His father, whom he hadn't seen in twenty-five years, had grown up in St. Louis, in the very neighborhood his firm was refurbishing. This proved to be a breakthrough in his career, and it helped propel him to opening his own firm several years later.

The point is that people tend to find the required discipline when the project is an endeavor they care about. See your current job as a perfectly suitable place to begin caring. As I've said before, this job is your career, at least for the time being.

Uproot Procrastination with Reward Systems

Some people find it infernally hard to force themselves to confront unpleasant tasks, whereas other, luckier folks just accept the discomfort, roll up their sleeves, and get it over with. I won't try to analyze the source of the problem for the resistant ones; after all, I'm not a psychologist, and the causes no doubt vary widely. But after seeing too many people wipe out, career-wise, because of their self-sabotaging time issues, I urge anyone who faces the problem to do whatever it takes to get over it.

The entire point of to-do lists and priority planning is to overcome the natural tendency to procrastinate, so if you take such steps and still manage to spin your wheels, there might be a more serious problem at play. You might be contending with fear issues—fear of success, of failure, of change, of self-exposure, and so on. If so, then I must reiterate the advice I emphasized in an earlier chapter: Get over it! When you get right down to it, no one really cares about your feelings, about what demons are shattering windshields in your hyperactive mind. What they care about are results. The workplace doesn't

DO OR DIE

Conceiving of deadlines in black-and-white terms is the best thing you can do for yourself.

A journalist friend of mine told me the most important educational experience he ever had was when he took an investigative reporting course in college. According to him, the professor was very smart, a talented writer, a dynamic teacher, a great person—and "a total hard-ass when it came to grading." On the first day of class, she told the students that they had three writing assignments that together would make up 70 percent of their grade. (The other 30 percent consisted of attendance and class participation.)

He quoted her: "Consider the due dates for these three writing assignments to be newsroom deadlines. If you miss any one of them, you will instantly fail my course. No exceptions. Even if you're a better writer than Hemingway."

Maybe that seems harsh, but she had a lesson to teach, and that's how she did it. And it worked. My friend has been a freelance journalist for seventeen years and has never missed a single deadline.

seem as heartless as, say, the military, but in truth it might even be more do-or-die. At least military people try at all costs to not leave their wounded behind. On the job, I wouldn't count on such compassion.

In other words, if you have a problem, find a solution. If a lack of concrete skills is the issue, then enroll in one of the many time-management courses offered at community colleges, job-training centers, and so on. Resources are available. If you think it would help to pay for a productivity-training coach for an hour or two a week for a few months, do it. There are more options than you can shake a pink slip at, so don't let the situation degenerate if you know there's a problem.

The point of devising a system that makes priorities crystal clear is that you can't lie to yourself while you procrastinate. Many people convince themselves that as long as they're doing something work-related they're not goofing off. But this is hogwash. If you're supposed to be writing a report about Middle East oil reserves, then reading an article about on-line brokerages is not bringing you closer to completing your assigned task.

The best systems for overcoming procrastination that I've seen are reward-based. You make deals with yourself—for example, when you complete the draft of the report, you can buy yourself that coveted CD. And you can try horse-trading items within your own schedule. If you're a fitness freak, then you can make gym time contingent on accomplishing a more odious task, such as replying to the thirty-eight e-mails that have gathered over the previous week in your in-box folder. The purpose of a reward-based system is not to make all accomplishments contingent on bribery, as if you were a lab chimp. Rather, the point is to develop better habits. Setting up positive associations with task fulfillment is a temporary training method. It does rely on positive reinforcement—the same as lab work does—but then, nearly all motivation seems to come down to such paybacks.

FOR YOUR OWN SAFETY

The most vital and strategically critical information of all is anything that pertains to you. It comes in many forms: a performance review, a note of thanks for an especially well written report, memos of your own to your supervisor describing the situation behind an unsuccessful project, or that supervisor's unfairly critical and cutting reaction. Everything that has any relation to your job performance is crucial stuff. Keep a separate folder of all such materials, copies if not the original documents, at home. You can use these materials to specifically justify your request for a substantial raise or a promotion—dates, details, and quotes will help you draft an effective memo to jog the memory of your supervisor. And in the

It's all too easy to procrastinate instead of doing tedious tasks, such as the paperwork for the company trip you took a few weeks ago. One solution of sorts is to schedule your day so you alternate the drudgery with more inspiring activities. For example, you could structure this particular day so the business trip paperwork is merely a way station between a brainstorming session with one of your idea people and a business lunch with a key client.

Sometimes the most important move you can make is to remove yourself from distraction. Working at home can help,

event of trouble, you want as much documentation as possible.

This information can potentially save your job —if, for example, one memo from your manager could easily be construed as sexist, top management might think twice about allowing this manager to summarily dismiss you.

And when you're ready to move on to another job, it's good to have a portfolio of complimentary materials assembled beforehand.

Also, in any situation that can go badly for you —for example, say you're called upon to mollify an irate and volatile client—make sure to take detailed notes of everything that happens, with the date and time of each conversation. If you can transcribe precise quotes, all the better. In the case of a dispute, your presentation of exact data will strengthen your viewpoint considerably.

as can going to work in an empty conference room on a different floor where no one will come and bug you. Laptops are especially effective, as is sequestering yourself, especially if you fancy listening to quiet music as you work. With a pair of headphones and a laptop screen, you're suspended in a sensory cocoon.

Incorporate Flexibility

Unless your personality is inflexible (and you're happy to remain that way), any system designed to help you accomplish your goals should be "flexibility friendly." A lack of leeway in handling situations stifles creativity—just as you'd expect it to. And the first kind of flexibility I'm referring to here is the system itself—as I mentioned, different strokes for different folks. One size definitely does not fit all. Some people do phenomenally well in life by keeping all their schedules and lists upstairs. Other people need to dot every *i* and cross every *t* on their action lists before they feel it's safe to leave the house.

The essential factor is that your system be tailored to your style. For example, I recommend later down in this chapter that you try to keep your desk and work space as uncluttered as possible. But it would be absurd to assert that this is a precondition for success. Many of my professional acquaintances maintain a fairly clutter-free environment. However, some of the most gifted and accomplished people I've ever met dwell, at work and at home, in a tornado-scape of papers and books and floppy disks. Furthermore, among these people, some can locate even a minute morsel of information in a nanosecond, whereas others spend an hour a day searching for their misplaced keys and wallet.

It's wise to leave some unscheduled time in your daily plan, because whether or not you budgeted for it, you're going to need some. Fires crop up all the time at work, and when one needs dousing you can't very well explain to the workers involved that your schedule doesn't permit you to help. Emergencies occur, distractions and interruptions happen. Don't try to "micro-second-manage" your time or else the normal entropy of existence will drive you batty. Also, some maneuvering room in your schedule makes it easier to rearrange tasks and activities.

Take Occasional Breaks

Other than when you're watching a (good) movie, sitting immobile in one place for several hours is uncomfortable, much more likely to induce restlessness than concentration. The same is true of work seats; on the physical plane, you need to get up and move around, stretch your limbs, move a little, get the blood flowing.

YOU ARE WHAT YOU SIT IN

Since I was raised in the furniture industry, I'm especially attuned in to the importance of good chairs for employee productivity. It's common sense, and I've seen the results at companies that upgrade their seating. Some of the leading office chair brands are Steelcase, Knoll, Herman Miller, K.I., Haworth, Kimball, Davis, and Vitra.

The owner of a Web-based company in the Boston area made an extraordinarily smart move by deciding to buy Herman Miller Aeron chairs for everyone at the company. It's true that these wonders cost about $800 each; however, that could well be the best human resource investment he ever makes. These analysts and researchers spend an average of seven hours a day actually in their seat. By purchasing one of the world's most coveted and most ergonomic office chairs, the entrepreneur contributed directly to their well-being—and his company's.

It's wise to "take your body for a walk" every hour, for at least five minutes. (And no, a thirty-minute lunch does not qualify as six hours' worth of stretch breaks.) Even if you're able to become thoroughly immersed in your work and hardly look up all day, your body and your psyche need occasional breaks.

Time Off Is Essential

As most of us know, all work and no play does not make Jack a dull boy. Rather, it turns Jack into a raving lunatic. To maintain your own sanity—and a high level of quality at work—you must take time off. It's the only way to prevent burnout.

Also: Why do you go to work? Is it just to make the money to sustain you so you can go back to work again? Most likely, other areas of your life are at least as important to you as work, and working is how you can support these pursuits.

Perhaps half the people I know claim they would sacrifice some pay for more time off. And yet many of these people can't even leave it all behind when they get away. They believe the world will implode if they don't call the office every other day. If you are lying on a beach in the Caribbean but thinking about your office at Forty-fourth Street and Seventh Avenue, then you're only halfway on vacation.

Vacations. It's a bad sign when someone is neglecting to take a vacation—even of the halfway variety. Forfeiting the chance to change your routine, scenery, and normal activities for at least a couple of weeks a year is very unhealthy. If you're a Nobel Prize–seeking biologist on the trail of a cure for diabetes, OK, skip the vacation. But anything short of that, you'll be a prime candidate for burnout. In terms of work, you'll do a far better job if you leave it behind periodically.

People who skip vacations seem like they're enslaved to their work. They call themselves workaholics, as if that makes it all right. But workaholism is an illness. I've seen it destroy a lot of marriages and leave emotionally scarred children in its wake.

Even if you live for your work, you need some time away—and preferably something better than a "I did things around the house" stint, which doesn't even qualify as a true vacation. There has to be more to your life than work. I know a lot of very successful businesspeople who are avid vacationers. Many have traveled all over the planet, seeking out culture, adventure sports, hedonism, or spirituality.

Mental Health Days or Extra Sick Days. A lot of people have asked me what I think about "mental health days." Well, calling in sick when you're healthy is, in essence, playing hooky. It's lying. On that level, it's not permissible. But if you truly need a true mental health day—that is, you need a day to depressurize or else you might melt down—then it's in everyone's interest for you to take that step, permissible or not.

But, someone asked me, what about taking a day off just to enjoy life a little when things are slow at work and you're caught up on everything? I'd say this is hardly a capital offense under those circumstances, but many bosses would still fire you if they found out, and they would be within their rights. So, you make your choices and you take your chances. Besides, at every job you can find a way to be productive and helpful to the business when you're "caught up" with your regular workload.

As for the practice of making sure to take all the allotted sick days, that's really pushing it. If you work at a small company, then I believe it's taking advantage of the proprietor. But at a corporation, someone could argue, it's foolish not to take what you can get because the corporation would fire you in a flash just to save a few bucks. That's true, they would; but the point is whether you could advance your own cause by being at work. Ambitious employees rarely stoop to this practice.

. . . and Space

Work space management is right up there with time management in importance. No matter how free-form or casual your personal style, your work area should always be organized and reasonably orderly. There are many benefits to doing so, and no downside. I don't buy it when folks say, "I can't work in a space that's too tidy." Of course they can. If you can get work done at a disorganized desk with papers and magazines stacked all over the cubicle, then you'll probably be even more efficient if you have a little more room to stretch out your thoughts. If you think you need some disorganization to be creative, then look inside your mind—we're all jammed with layer upon layer of ideas, opinions, impressions, hunches, and so on. The expression "A neat desk is a sign of an empty mind" is just a pithy self-excuse contrived by a clever slob.

Well-organized doesn't mean squeaky-clean. What it does mean is:

► You know where everything is.

► Everything has a place—books, files, supplies, your gym bag, and so on.

► Mobility is unimpeded—there are no stacks of papers on the floor.

► You can access whatever you need with a minimum of effort.

► There's not an excess of "visual clutter."

► If someone else needs to locate some material, they could figure out where it is on their own or with a few quick directions from you.

THE ERGONOMICALLY CORRECT WORK SPACE

When your work space fits you like well-tailored clothes, you're free to work at your optimal productivity level. I call this a state of "ergonomically correct working." Just as you need to properly set a chair's lumbar support to make it ergonomically sound, your office is like that chair writ large. The farther you fall short of this ideal, the less productive you're likely to be.

How do you attain this state of grace? By positioning all your work implements—furniture, computer, files, phone, and so on—so that you nearly never have to interrupt your thoughts or activities to rearrange things or "hunt" for some item or paperwork.

ERGONOMICS TIPS

Discomfort is efficiency's greatest enemy. To be truly well organized, your work space must be set up for comfort. Your computer keyboard and mouse need to be at the right height.

Chairs are crucial. Without being obsessive about it, you should be sure you have a comfortable chair. If the company doesn't provide one that's good enough, and refuses to purchase a better one (which it's worth asking for), then at least bring in your own lumbar support to improve the chair's ergonomics.

Another biggie is the telephone. If your job entails substantial phone time, you should get your-

Meanwhile, the failure to maintain an organized work space undermines productivity in at least three major ways:

It translates directly into lost time. Space and time are directly connected. If you spend even 20 minutes a day tracking down some file, document, or publication, that adds up, big time—to the tune of, say, 4,800 minutes a year ... 80 hours ... nearly 2 full workweeks! No, such efficiency won't buy you an extra eight days of vacation, but it will give you back a sizable chunk of personal time. Little by little adds up to big.

It sends the wrong message to the other employees—and, more important, to yourself. What it says when your space is a chaotic

self a headset. This is especially true if you need to take notes at the same time (as most people do). Headsets free up your hand, free you from neck strain, and allow you to focus more completely on the conversation. Plantronics specializes in this type of equipment, but Radio Shack makes some inexpensive units that work just fine. (There are models that you just stick in your ear that serve as both microphone and speaker, but they don't work well for everyone.) If your company won't spring for it, then you should buy your own. We're not talking a lot of money for a basic model, and they can make a huge improvement in your physical comfort and ease.

mess is that you're incapable of getting your act together—and, therefore, that you're probably incompetent. There's nothing dignified or professional about working at a desk where the day's mail quickly gets buried in a landslide of other paperwork. Chances are good that you'll fail to reply to letters in a timely fashion, or take necessary actions when they're required. Nobody could safely assume you'd come through for them in a pinch if you can't even keep your work space tidy. Also, it's not a comfortable environment for other employees to visit for a quick meeting; most face-to-face meetings between coworkers happen with one sitting at the extra chair in the other's cubicle. That's not a healthy option for the person with distracting piles of work everywhere; in fact, it might be hard to clear the space for someone else to sit. Another point is that it often makes other workers uncomfortable when one of their cohorts has a cubicle or office that looks as if it's been hit by a tornado. It taints the atmosphere and makes it seem like the company is a little out of control.

It makes it impossible for others to access information. No one other than you has a prayer of finding materials in a disarrayed office. What happens if you get hit by a bus and have to convalesce for a month? Other workers will need to access papers and other items. Even if you're able to provide "directions" by phone, you'll cost the company many, many hours of other employees' wasted productivity.

The Fifteen-Second Rule

One radio caller asked me this very good question: How much is enough? That is, how do you know when you're sufficiently well organized? The answer: When you don't have to make people wait.

For example, when you're on the phone with a client and you need to pluck a file and check some figures so you sound like you know exactly what you're talking about. It's bad form to tell this person you'll get back to them after you "track the information down." Your files aren't fugitives; they're your raw materials and your tools! Imagine if a police officer had to go rummaging through the glove compartment whenever he needed to cuff a suspect.

My rule of thumb is that you should be able to put your hands on any materials within fifteen seconds. (If you have a slow computer, we can make allowances for that.) You should be able to stall a client on the phone for that long by asking one tangential question. By then, you should have what you need.

There's a larger point here: Never make yourself wait for more than fifteen seconds to find something. Your time is too valuable to waste it in silly ways such as rummaging around your office.

How to Clear a Desk

Your desk is your immediate work zone, and it's especially important to keep it free of junk. In fact, a lot of people find it easiest to work on a project if they've cleared everything off the desk surface that's not related to the task at hand. The idea isn't to give your body elbowroom, but rather to avoid obstructing your brain. (Though the physical elbowroom is nice as well, since a cramped body usually creates a cramped mind.)

The way to establish a state of grace for your desk is simple: Make sure that everything has a place it belongs other than on your desktop. That's like saying the way to be thin is not to weigh too much, right? Not quite. It's easier to line up books and stack files on your desk than finding a place to assign incoming materials, and I'm saying you shouldn't fall into that habit. Obviously, the desk is the right place for tools you use constantly—such as, say, your tape dispenser.

And what's with the junk in your desk drawers? It's tempting to toss in anything you think might come in handy some time. So you have a few hundred coffee swizzlers, for example, and five mouse pads from Amazon.com. And that's just the beginning. In the paper drawer are dozens of letters you never replied to, offers for professional subscriptions, and so on.

The mission: Clear out all the junk and start from scratch; set up a system and then stick with the program. You'll need to go through the whole cubicle or office—it doesn't make sense to tackle just your desk; your system should encompass all your materials, not just the desk-based stuff. If the situation is badly out of hand, the best idea is usually to come in over the weekend so you can focus on getting organized without interruption. If you succeed in transforming work space chaos into order, it's one of the best-invested weekend days you'll ever spend.

Set aside some quality time to purge and reorganize your desk and office/cubicle. Here's an action plan you can adopt and modify as befits your space constraints and working style:

- Empty all your drawers. Throw (or give) away anything that you haven't used for six months (unless it serves a very specific purpose, such as the handheld minicassette recorder you really do bring to the annual trade convention).
- Blast through magazines, ruthlessly. Scan the tables of contents. Unless there's a piece that's essential to your work, toss or reroute the issue.
- File every piece of paper that you can. Keep a one-page written list of the files you need to deal with after this clean-up project.
- Toss every bit of paper you possibly can. Set aside, in two respective folders, those with useful contact info or anything pertaining to your job performance.
- Once you've jettisoned the flotsam, organize what's left for accessibility: Place the most important desk

items in the top drawers and active-project files within easy reach of your telephone and your computer station. Any reference works you use on a regular basis— industry directories, dictionaries, order-in pizza menus —should be near at hand.

▸ Have one or (at most) two "set-aside spaces"—a place to put papers you want to return to or books you need to consult later but where they're not cluttering up your desk surface.

▸ If you have a lot of knickknacks on your desk or shelves, the office-space purge is a great opportunity to get rid of some. You'll have less to distract you if you do and you'll appear more professional.

Get in the Habit

Once you've organized your space, the challenge is to keep from mucking it all up again. To prevent that, you need to perfect a system for handling all incoming materials—paperwork, books, supplies, coats, packages of personal items you buy during lunch, whatever. And above all, stick to it. Don't let it disintegrate so that it's no longer functional—for instance, don't just start stacking all your to-do materials in one pile where you can forget about it. One habit to avoid, in fact, is stacking; it's a sure way to misplace important materials and lose time searching.

An incredibly important habit for avoiding clutter buildup is to route periodicals as quickly as you can. When magazines hit your in box, move them along by the next day. Make a copy of whatever you want to keep first (assuming your company has a group subscription to that magazine, of course).

But don't interrupt your work schedule to read them; factor in a half-hour at the end or beginning of the day to handle all such materials. Also, when new catalogs or directories arrive, immediately recycle the old one (after flipping through just to be sure you don't toss away any important notes you've jotted).

Also, think of your floor as off-limits. It's like a basement: Once you deposit things down there, they rarely make it back up to desk level. Same thing for the tops of bookcases—it's the attic of your office.

Info-Management: Cut the Glut

In the current era, managing your time or organizing your work space requires you to deal with the information glut every day. Of course, the problem is much worse with regard to time rather than space, especially now that an ocean of information can be pumped in and deluge any size office through a single high-speed, dedicated, digital line.

You gather and assimilate a lot of information to do your job. But there's no way you can possibly keep up with all the information out there (you can go nuts trying). Therefore, you must devise a system that suits your style and manages the flow so you learn what you need to without being over-whelmed by everything else. I'm meeting more and more people who are literally obsessed with information—not only are employees spending half their time chasing after informa-tion, but they're taking up half their work space hoarding it.

Obviously, if you don't have a system for dealing with the information flow, you're sunk. The first thing you need to do is

GIVE THEM THE BUSINESS CARD

Unfortunately, some basic elements of professionalism seem to be falling by the wayside. For example, an important adjunct to managing data about other people is being able to provide your own coordinates to them. Fortunately, there exists a simple, effective, time-tested technology for this: the business card. Too many employees, and especially younger ones, neglect to carry these. (I've even encountered cardless professionals in the middle of trade shows!) When someone asks for your card, the answer should never be "I don't have one with me." Nothing makes a worse impression. If you're caught empty-handed, in fact, always say something like "I just gave away my last one a few minutes ago" to try to cover up your oversight.

Stuff a bunch into every purse, laptop carrying case, suit jacket, pants pocket that you own. This way, you're unlikely to "accidentally run out" of cards. Always order more than you need, and dispense them freely. You never know when or where they might come in handy.

home in on the type of information you really need, because this will help you focus your info-gathering efforts. Information breaks down into the following categories:

► Your schedule, to-do lists, and other personal planning tools.

- ▶ Information about your current and upcoming projects.
- ▶ Contact info on everyone you know or meet, especially clients and professional connections.
- ▶ Department and company intelligence, including the status of projects, contents of memos and reports, and anything you find out or hear about coworkers.
- ▶ Industry issues, such as what the competition is doing, new developments in technology, and business conditions.
- ▶ General knowledge—everything that helps you do a better job and interact with coworkers and clients.

If your job entails knowing everything about everybody—as mine does—that means a lot of airtime, talking with people "in the know." But if you work at an HMO, for example, your most important subjects might include government regulations, information about competing organizations, and perhaps scientific or technology news. For most employees, the top four categories listed are the ones they have to worry about most. The last two are like "extra credit": If you can manage it, great, but it's not necessary for success.

The most essential type of information comprises basic data—about people, times, places, and events. This is stuff you should never accidentally lose or forget, so you need a place to take it down when you first encounter it. We'll start with that.

Hot Data Devices

The biggest sin in business is to forget an important meeting or appointment. Which is why we all need a system to record information on the spot. Even if you're young and sharp, when you're given important data—such as times and places—you must write it down. Don't tell me "Oh, I'll remember." Because eventually you will slip up. So don't be a big shot: Write it down.

These days, all you hear about are personal digital assistants (PDAs) and other portable electronic devices, but there are other good options too. The main thing is that your system is foolproof. So if you use a PDA, always carry it with you and be sure to download the information onto your main computer. If you carry a notepad, then make sure to have a pen too, and make sure to transfer the information to its proper place, such as your calendar back at the office. Another requirement is that your system be as simple as possible. This reduces the likelihood of making errors and increases the likelihood you'll stick with your system and not cut corners.

If you believe the media, you'd think the whole world has gone digital, but that's a distortion. Sure, at Internet companies where the average age is twenty-four, everyone probably uses PDAs. But in the rest of the world, which is the majority of the workplace, only a small percentage of employees use those devices. Everyone else is getting by just fine with Daytimers and Filofaxes.

I also carry what I call my Magic Notebook, a bound notebook (i.e., the pages can't be torn out like a spiral notebook's) with the black marble pattern on the cover—the type we used in grade school. Each year, I go through a number of these, which I save for reference and record-keeping. In these notebooks I write down everything I need to remember—contacts, facts, finances, everything. At meetings, this is where my notes go. The information is imprinted permanently, in

VITAL STATISTICS

In business, I've found that it's especially important to remember people's birthdays. If you have an assistant, for example, do not under any circumstances forget his or her birthday. There's always someone in the office who remembers, and you look awfully bad when that someone drops a "Happy Birthday!" on your secretary or officemate when you're forgotten about it.

Mentioning it is better than nothing, but taking someone to lunch is the better way to go if the person is important to you at work. People are very sensitive about their birthdays, even those who pretend they aren't. They remember who remembered. Being the kind of person who remembers birthdays can pay dividends in the business world.

One caveat: Don't expect such birthday consideration in return. People forget.

one place. It's never accidentally deleted, and unlike my computer it never crashes. (I'm extremely aware of its whereabouts whenever I have it with me.)

Before I adopted this tool I had loose papers everywhere, and I spent at least half an hour a day searching for notes from various conversations. That problem disappeared; a two-hundred-page hard-backed notebook is hard to misplace. Also, I used to jot down a lot of trivial information, whereas in the

Magic Notebook I include only what counts. I've gotten great at summarizing, because I'm constantly referring to this book, and I don't want to wade through blather. The Magic Notebook system works well for others too, including GE chairman Jack Welch, who uses the exact same kind of notebook.

What matters isn't the level of technology, but whether your system is efficient for you. The most eccentric example I know is a gentleman who has been an executive VP at a design agency for many years. After he and I shook hands at industry gatherings, I'd notice later that my hand had blue streaks on it. Finally, I asked him about this, and he held up his palm so I could see it. On it were written six phone numbers. That was his system: When he'd get a new number, he'd scrawl it on his hand so he was sure to copy it down later in his Rolodex.

If you're thirty-five or under, any low-tech solution might sound backward. For anyone who's already comfortable using a PDA, I can certainly understand their value. As calendars and contact books, they're terrific. But they're not great for writing involved notes. The application for which the PDAs really shine is scheduling future appointments. A forty-one-year-old manager at a Web research company—the "token old guy," as he puts it—told me that when he's at meetings and the parties decide to meet again later, "out come their handy-dandy PDAs, and they can 'ink' it in. Me, I just write a note and say I'll get back to them if the timing's a problem."

Other methods I've seen include mini-recorders and leaving voice mails (or sending e-mails) for oneself. All that matters is that you remember. As I tell trainees at my own company, the only wrong way to remember is to forget.

Parallel Processing

A large percentage of our information these days is in digital form. On one hand, it's a great boon, especially for workers who manipulate data, images, or text. But it creates problems, too—such as the difficulty of coordinating digital information with hard copy. And because it's just as easy to get disorga-

---

PUBLISHING WITHOUT PERISHING

I've worked with many people in publishing. Professionals in that field either master the art of information processing or they become time-stress sufferers. Most of them have to cope with deluges of information just to get to their assigned tasks, let alone finish the work.

A friend of mine is the editorial director of a magazine published in New York, and she describes her position as nonstop information crossed with nonstop communication. To do her job, she speaks with and writes to thousands of people every year: reporters, writers, editors, outside experts, interview subjects, executives from her division's European owners, entertainers, politicians, intellectuals, and scientists. What's expected of her is that she always seem to be knowledgeable and intelligent—about everything. She is extremely bright, of course, but to do her job she has to absorb tons of information.

nized on a computer as it is in a filing cabinet, digital content must be as well organized as any other kind of information. If not, you waste time searching and perhaps make serious errors (when someone accidentally uses the wrong version of a spreadsheet, for example).

You want all your stored data, computerized and paper,

If she didn't have a well-honed system, there's no way she could pull it off. How does it work? Her assistant's main duties include separating important and unimportant correspondence—regular mail, e-mail, and voice mail. She also filters through periodicals and several Web sites, and highlights those pieces that my friend should read. My friend also has a couple of highly trusted confidants in the industry on whom she can count to cut through the trivia and give her the real deal on what's happening in the publishing world and business in general. She makes sure to cultivate correspondences with a diverse group of experts whom she can tap for insights when the occasion arises.

She also recommends selective speed-reading. "With novels, I read nice and slowly; it's only on vacation that I get a chance, and I want to savor it. But with professional materials, I blast through, watching for certain keywords. When I find something interesting I slow down quite a bit, to really take it in. A lot of times, whole articles can be summarized with a note or two. I'm big on notes."

organized the same way, in parallel systems. The goal is to concentrate all relevant data about a given subject in the smallest number of locations. If you segregate your information by client, for example, then assign a separate paper folder and hard-disk folder per client. If you already have different file-cabinet drawers assigned by function: finances, marketing, manuscripts, and such, then set up your hard drive in a parallel fashion.

Perhaps you'll find the way you organize material on your PC is better than the system you've implemented with paper content. In that case, redo your paper system; it's a hassle, sure, but it's worth it. On all your paper files, write down the corresponding computer files and folders.

Make sure you include e-mails in your storage system. Don't let them just sit in your e-mail program; transfer them to the dedicated project or client folders on your hard disk. Some people copy e-mail messages into word-processing files to make them easier to access once they're stored; you can label the files very specifically—for instance, "2.26.00-Client Name-Price Quote"—so you can locate key e-mails in a flash (and satisfy the fifteen-second rule).

Another tip: Information is often easier to work with in paper form than on a computer monitor. Spatially, you can take in more at once when it's spread on a surface, rather than bouncing from one computer screen to another (though this has its advantages too, it depends on how your brain works and what you're working on). A lot of people find that extensive monitor reading strains the eyes. And it's much easier to take notes on paper.

way to go! and *a wrong turn!* Brenda took organization

to extremes. A project manager for an on-line gaming company, she spent most of her work time making beautiful flow charts and schedules. She instituted a color-coding system for the office master files, so that anyone from any department knew that contracts would always be in yellow folders and invoices and payment stubs would always be in green "money" folders. The summer interns could be instructed to retrieve a yellow or green or red or blue file from a client folder, and ten times out of ten, the right folder came back out of the filing cabinet. Brenda created elegant forms for people in her own and other departments to fill out— transmission forms, contract payment term forms, invoice forms, games to production forms. She filled huge, tabbed binders with chronologically ordered correspondence and interoffice memos. She invented far more systems than her four-person department—and twenty-five-person company— really needed. And she spent so much time revising schedules that no project ever had a chance of being delivered on time, because with all the revisions it was impossible to know what the real deadlines were. Brenda's efforts are an example of how too much of a good thing can become toxic. When organizing becomes an end in itself, the real goals of an organization are eclipsed.

Don't Lose It

One last point about managing information: *Back up your hard drive!* A disk crash can be truly tragic. If you lose six months of work, you've lost six months of your life in a way. It's not a detail; it's an absolute requirement. Don't think it won't happen to you, because one day it will. And afterward you'll be an evangelist about this too. Don't wait for it to happen to you. Also, don't rely on the automatic system at work unless you know it's 100 percent up to snuff—that is, it's been tested, and tested recently. I've heard dozens of woeful tales about workplace system crashes where the fail-safe system failed to save anyone's data.

Make sure you have a foolproof system in place, and that you use it every single day without fail. Disk crashes can't be prevented, but losing more than a few hours of work can be. Employees I know who ignored the peril and ended up losing a huge amount of material said nothing has made them feel so stupid.

7

Beyond the Job:
Career Talk

TAKEN TOGETHER, THE PREVIOUS CHAPTERS
prepare you to be a formidable player in the work
game. You have the insights, tactics, and strategies
to navigate workplace politics, wield political influence, and make it through the day with your
spirit and sanity intact. You're prepared to maintain a steady and fairly smooth course, and with
some luck you'll move ahead over time.

But if your intention is to make rapid and certain progress—that is, to take an active, aggressive
approach to your professional advancement—
then extra efforts are required. Instead of merely
biding time and accepting what comes your way,
make your own luck. Don't just pounce on oppor-

tunities, create them. When favorable attention shines your way, don't merely bask in the glory, leverage that glory and go for more. This chapter shows how to capitalize on both challenges and opportunities to surge forward in your career.

Over the years, I've seen a lot of employees (including those who've worked for me) drop the ball at make-or-break moments on the job, situations in which they could either make a quantum leap forward or fall flat. Too often, folks just miss opportunities, either because they weren't willing to take a chance or they simply didn't recognize the possibilities. I've also seen employees miss the boat in damage-control situations. What many people don't realize is that if you handle a difficult situation—even one of your own making—with dignity, you can actually gain kudos rather than lose face.

In broad terms, there are four key principles that when applied on the job, inevitably advance your position and career. And they are:

Share the credit. When the opportunity arises, not only should you avoid hogging the credit, but you can also afford to be a little "overgenerous" in passing the credit around.

Be accountable. Own up to your responsibility—mistakes and all. When you admit an error, do it promptly and with dignity. And don't ever take the fall for other peoples' slip-ups.

Keep cool in a crisis. Workplace explosions are best avoided, but when you can't escape the fray, then at least come out of the situation looking like one of the strong ones.

Articulate your ambitions. "You have to be in it to win it" applies perfectly to career development. If you're not content to stand still, then you need to let management know that you're in the running.

Share the Credit

It's essential that you receive acknowledgment for your work accomplishments. If not, then your efforts aren't doing you any good. After all, you're not going to work every day just to feel altruistic; you're trying to make a living, do well, build strategic relationships, get raises, and move ahead. None of that is likely at all unless you're given the credit you're due. If this isn't happening, you need to take immediate steps to change that.

Credit Can Take Many Forms
It's always a valuable feather when you get a formal written acknowledgment. That's part of the purpose of the year-end performance review, but if possible, have your supervisor type out a separate memo or letter when you've accomplished something notable or performed especially well. Thank-you letters from appreciative clients are also excellent additions to your "credit portfolio," not just for the long term but also as items to show your manager. Whenever you're moving on from a job, and assuming the passing is amicable, ask for written recommendations from all the managers you admire or who have clout.

Another excellent type of credit currency is an announce-

SHUNNING CREDIT
GETS YOU EVEN MORE

The next step beyond sharing credit is shunning it. I don't mean refusing it when you haven't earned it (as I've mentioned above), but forfeiting some of the credit that's rightfully yours. This is a matter of degree. If you claim you didn't accomplish something that you did, for example, this veers into serious dishonesty. But usually, shunning credit means you drastically downplay your contribution for the sake of promoting what others did.

What does this accomplish? It fortifies your role as a benevolent leader among those to whom you deflected the credit. While it might seem to skirt the edge of altruism, it's actually a strategic move that gives you a lot of power with the people you've helped. (Of course, if the chemistry

ment at a department or company meeting about your good work. Likewise, being written up in the company newsletter is perfect—everyone in the organization will know, and they're likely to reread it several times. As mentioned earlier, keep a file at home containing any documents relating to your work performance.

And remember the power of the grapevine. In the midst of a project, everyone knows who's doing what; coworkers are also likely to know the outcome of any project or program. It's your responsibility to make sure that the story circulates when

among the employees is "off," such behavior can breed resentment.)

The fact is, management and coworkers nearly always know the real deal. If you were the brains behind a project, you'll be tapped for the next important project too. When you sincerely shun credit, it strongly suggests the following:

▶ You're serious about your profession. You're in it for the challenge, not just the payoff.

▶ You expect a lot more credit and honor to come your way, which is why you don't have to grasp at the current batch.

▶ You're not even close to realizing your full potential yet. This feat was just a warm-up for greater accomplishments.

▶ You're a true team player, as opposed to most people who just pay lip service to the idea.

you do something well—and that the story is accurate. This tends to be part of the normal cycle at most companies. It would be the sign of a problem if it weren't commonly known when someone accomplishes something exceptional.

Share the wealth. Hopefully, you're situated at a job where you're credited for any and all achievements. In such cases, you want to use this credit strategically. The way to do that is to spread it around. Credit isn't infinite; there's only so much to go around for any specific project. But it is surprisingly expandable. There's more of it to go around than you think.

Sharing credit for your accomplishments makes everyone feel favorably disposed toward you. And the more obvious it is that you're responsible for this achievement, whether it was landing a big contract or completing a Web site redesign or whatever, the better it makes you look when you spread the credit. As long as there's no ambiguity about who the real hero is, you've nothing to lose—and loads of goodwill and esteem to gain. When you include other employees in taking credit for a project, you establish an identity as a "team player." At the same time, by being the one who "shares" the credit, you demonstrate that most of the credit is yours.

Knowing how to spread the wealth is especially important for new or young executives. You're already on an upward path, so you can afford to be modest. It's an excellent way to fortify existing affiliations and demonstrate to everyone that you are a gracious ally. Plus, bestowing credit on your subordinates is invaluable in securing their loyalty. Use little events—staff meetings, going-away parties, anything—to offer some public honor to others.

As with anything you do in the work arena, there's more to sharing credit than meets the eye. The following guidelines will help reflect more glory your way while bolstering your work relationships.

▶ If you're given credit that you truly don't deserve, and there's a reasonable chance that this fact will come to light, then be insistent on redirecting the credit to the worthy party or parties. By doing so, you demonstrate that any praise you accept in the future (or have in the past) was justified: "I don't need to take credit for anyone else's deeds; I have enough of my own." If, however, you're unduly credited for something where the truth is not likely to surface (you made a strategic business decision based strictly on advice from a former employee), then just accept it—without playing it up.

▸ Be clear on the difference between thanking and sharing credit. Thanking is merely expressing gratitude for help; sharing credit is explicitly crediting someone for contributing to a successful outcome. It's always good to thank anyone who helps you out on a task or project, even if his or her contributions were minor. But that's not the same as sharing credit. Any expression of gratitude should be sincere. Remember that you can't take a "thank you" back.

▸ Make sure you can afford to be magnanimous. For starters, be sure your work has been thoroughly well received; if some important company managers are backhanded in their endorsement, you might not have scored a big enough hit to make any sweeping gestures. Every little achievement doesn't merit a generous reaction from you.

▸ Don't heap false praise. The recipients will know it's bunk, and so will everyone else.

▸ When you give praise, do so generously. In situations where others are due legitimate accolades, lay them on thick and heavy. Even if you attribute all the well-executed moves and ideas to others, the core achievement will glow brightly in your corner.

▸ Put it in writing. People are especially appreciative when they're given documentation. E-mail makes this extremely easy.

Bosses—A Two-Way Street

Credit generally comes from above you in the company chart. And the smart employee always gives back some of that largesse to its source. This is a healthy reciprocity. So the first person in line for your praise is always your own supervisor. Don't neglect this pathway, because your relationship with your supervisor is vital to your credit economy. Anything you can do to keep the channel in tiptop shape is wise.

I received the following e-mail from a listener:

> *Dear Stephen,*
> *My manager and I are working together on a major long-term project that involves a lot of traveling. We're constantly meeting new people and making professional intro-ductions. Please tell me, what's the best way to define our roles? For example, do I call him my executive supervisor (which is the official title back at headquarters), even though that sounds bizarre? And how should a supervisor introduce his or her subordinate to new business acquaintances? He seems to be no more comfortable than I am with this chronic issue.*

My answer to this is: Call him "my boss." Some managers might object, but it's generally just for show. Actually, they appreciate it. They worked hard (perhaps) to get where they are, and they enjoy the recognition. Plus, once it's clear who's answering to whom, your new acquaintances know how to direct questions. I would also recommend using the "boss" tag at the office. Not so often that it's grating, but enough to let your supervisor know that you recognize the corporate "class system." If you have to ask for a favor, don't forget to introduce the question with a nice respectful "boss." Sure, it's manipulative—that's why you should do it. It's very seductive to be called boss. My first manager objected, but I persisted because I knew the objections weren't sincere; he just felt morally obligated to discourage the master/serf dynamic.

Now, as for how your "boss" should introduce you, it's always appropriate for your manager to say you and he "work together." It's bad form for a manager, or even a business owner, to refer to someone as "my employee" or to say a person "works for me." Managers are expected to be a little generous with this nomenclature because they can afford to, but it's also real—the people all do work together, that's the bottom line. Even if one person calls the shots most of the time, you're still colleagues.

It's symmetrical: The supervisor wants the worker to show respect for him or her as a boss, and the worker wants the supervisor to demonstrate respect for the worker as a human being.

By the same token, always try to make your manager look good and show respect. Not only is it essential for your mutual relationship, but it also shows that you're not too arrogant to remember your place in the pecking order. Don't worry that it'll tarnish your sheen to pay your respects to your supervisor. As you rack up successes, it becomes crystal clear that you're a star.

Sometimes the Boss Is a Logjam in the Credit Pipeline

One serious problem a lot of employees face is having a manager who's too insecure or negligent to dispense encouragement, thanks, congratulations, public acknowledgment, written praise, or any other tangible evidence of an employee's achievements. (I've noticed that credit sharing is often a major source of contention in manager/subordinate situations where both parties are female. A woman manager sharing the credit with a female underling is the most problematic of the gender combinations. Perhaps it's a lingering side effect of the historical restrictions imposed on women in the corporate world.)

If you see that your own boss is tightfisted when it comes to acknowledgments, it's up to you to take steps to overcome this scarcity. First, speak to your supervisor, with specific requests for recognition of your accomplishments. (Make sure you don't oversell what you've achieved, of course.) A good tack to take with your supervisor is to claim you realize he or she is busy, but you really value the person's commendation— and mention that you also realize that your accomplishments reflect well on his or her leadership.

If this doesn't do the trick, then you can try to use company channels to let people know what you've accomplished.

For example, you could ask the marketing VP to glance over your report to be sure you've adopted the precise "positioning message" the company is promoting.

If all else fails, you can ask to be transferred to another manager. If you're at the point where you're thinking of leaving the job anyway, you have little to lose.

Sometimes the Boss Diverts the Credit Flow Entirely

Unfortunately, some managers not only suppress their underlings' achievements but they even steal their employees' thunder. If your supervisor is taking direct credit for your work, you should either quit or change departments. There's no other

way to go!   I know a high-powered publicity agent who's virtually a kingmaker—or at least a celebrity-maker more than once. He and his business partner, who's ten years older than my acquaintance, have an amazing track record in the press agent world. The older agent has also been a screenwriter, television sitcom writer, and a novelist, whereas the younger one is a true publicity maven, whose expertise is getting press attention for his clients. The older partner has an enormous ego and a huge competitive streak. He throws a fit when clients don't openly acknowledge his work and thank him for it. The younger partner's attitude about credit is that the work speaks for itself. When I asked him about it, he said, "It's really not the credit that counts. It's producing successful publicity campaigns so we can continue to build our reputation." Those words indicate no lack of ego, but rather the presence of true self-confidence.

remedy when your supervisor is lying; this is not a person you can ever trust.

If you decide to go to upper management, make sure you have documentation that proves the work was yours. Even so,

---

way to go! Simon, an editorial director at a large publisher, spearheaded a market-research project for a new publication, which would be an offshoot of an existing magazine. Richard was the marketing manager who had buy-in to the project, but he resented the fact that it was an editorial executive rather than a marketer who was heading it up. (The reason was that the magazine was Simon's idea, and he had already devised a questionnaire and a research strategy; so top management put him in charge.) The survey went well, and the company decided to launch the publication. Simon heard that Richard was going around and implying that he had masterminded the whole project. When someone asked if it were true, Simon said, "No, Richard helped out by compiling the database, which was very useful because then I could focus my research on our prime demographics." Someone who'd heard from Richard that he'd captained the project questioned Simon further about this. He looked sincerely surprised. "No, Richard didn't direct any of the strategizing; but he did handle the statistical backend for the first phase of the project. Which, as I said, was a big help in getting the more complicated phase started." Simon had the truth on his side, and didn't need to engage in petty sniping. But he had no intention of giving up the credit that he'd earned. Had Richard not tried to pirate the glory, Simon would've very likely given Richard more credit than he'd earned, rather than to offhandedly reveal to colleagues that Richard was acting disgracefully.

---

the honchos may not be sympathetic. They could have their own reasons for keeping your supervisor on staff, and your complaint is an inconvenience that they'll choose to ignore. You'll either be fired or have to leave anyway. Other times, however, I've seen bosses get canned for their treachery—and I know of at least two cases where the whistle-blowing employee got the manager's job!

Deal with Interlopers

If another coworker, rather than a manager, is trying to steal your thunder, different techniques are required. Make sure you know what the imposter is claiming as his or her contribution. Then, when you discuss the project with people, you could present your competitor's role in an accurate but diminished light. This will counteract his exaggerations.

It's important that you not slight the other person's contribution too much; if you do, your credibility will be shot. By acknowledging the interloper's contribution in a reasonable and precise-sounding manner, yours will seem like the truthful voice.

Be Accountable

Whatever your position or level of experience, always be accountable and accept responsibility for your actions. This includes, of course, owning up to errors and admitting mistakes. Accountability is the basic building block of maturity and professionalism. It's simple: Accountable employees are trustworthy. Conversely, employees who shirk responsibility, instinctively pass the buck, blame everyone, or don't tell their managers what's going on are untrustworthy.

Among the most important elements of being accountable is acknowledging when you make a mistake. My advice is straightforward: When you make an error, admit it as quickly as possible so you and the other employees or managers involved can proceed. If remedial action is called for, then volunteer to provide it. Do whatever you can to reverse or avert any damage and move on.

One of the main reasons I've had to fire employees—and I've seen this happen in numerous companies—is for their refusal to acknowledge responsibility for a mistake. Nothing is more infuriating than when someone refuses to admit he or she was wrong, not merely because they seem dishonest, foolish, immature, and petty (though they do), but because this behavior often creates problems for others. These workers will go through contortions to avoid conceding that they're fallible. They'll lie, falsify results, "frame" their colleagues—everything except own up. Obviously, these people are severe liabilities to have around.

Young people who have entered the workforce in the past five years or so seem to be especially unwilling to admit when they've made mistakes. I've never noticed such a pronounced pattern in earlier cohorts. There's a tremendous amount of pressure to succeed—and fast—that is responsible for this tendency.

Everybody makes mistakes. You might forget to do something, or accidentally misplace some important information. It happens. Sometimes it's a judgment error—a magazine editor

wrong turn! Marcie was a new manager at a catering service with a growing client base. The company was situated in a competitive market where profit margins were exceptionally tight, and it was impressed on Marcie to be vigilant about avoiding cost overruns or unexpected outlays. One day Marcie took an order for a buffet dinner to be held several weeks later at a nearby corporate headquarters. The human resources employee who ordered the food explicitly told Marcie that there must be no peanut-based products in anything, because one of the company's senior executives was highly allergic. Marcie made a note and assured the HR employee that she'd take care of it. She didn't see a place on the form to enter the information on the invoice itself, so she intended to tell the head chef personally. Things got very busy at the caterer, and Marcie forgot to mention the peanut ban to the chef. Two days before the affair, the HR manager called Marcie to confirm everything was in order, and she asked Marcie about the peanuts. Instead of admitting her error, she assured the HR person that she'd taken care of that. Marcie did not want to admit her mistake to her employer, so instead she scanned the menu for the event herself, looking for signs of peanuts. What she didn't realize was that there were peanuts in the frosting of the chocolate cake. At the dinner, the allergic executive had some of the cake and had to be rushed to the emergency room in anaphylactic shock. There were terrible recriminations later, including the threat of a lawsuit. Marcie insisted she hadn't been told about the peanuts. The human resources worker insisted that Marcie had known—and her manager backed her up, because she'd been standing by the worker's desk during the follow-up phone call to Marcie. Of course, Marcie was fired.

decides to run a special "topical" report, and two of the publication's three direct competitors decide to cover the same subject (which was too obvious). Admit the error, correct any situation that needs remedying, and move on. Don't dissemble and don't lie to yourself.

Raising your hand to say "My mistake. I screwed up on that one" proves that you're a professional and you have the self-confidence to be up-front and honest. Your coworkers know you're for real, and not likely to backstab in order to get ahead. Ultimately, you gain. Plus, people don't lose time as you gum up the works trying to conceal the error, blame it on someone else, or justify it by persisting in your folly.

The point is to admit your goof-ups with dignity. Don't hang your head in shame, because then your manager and coworkers will treat you as if you deserve those feelings of worthlessness. And don't be arrogant, as if making a grand gesture gains you your peers' respect. Just be straightforward, with an attitude that says you'll be sure to avoid making the same mistake again, that you've learned something from the experience.

Employees who take calculated risks and then admit their mistakes are more valuable to me as an employer than those who always cleave to the safe and narrow in fear of "being wrong." Making errors is part of the learning curve; workers who are reluctant or refuse to acknowledge their mistakes generally don't learn much or grow. Nor do they tend to be the real go-getters. (And when they are, it's a dangerous combination.)

Don't Be the Fall Guy

It's one thing to admit your mistakes, but quite another to get nailed for other people's mess-ups. Employees who rarely accept responsibility for their mistakes often take advantage of the employee who raises his or her hand. Often when business situations go bad, there are several people whose judgment was at fault. Sometimes a shirker will say nothing as another employee acknowledges his or her errors, in which case it appears that the honest one was responsible for the entire problem. Or the shifty employee will claim that his or her lapse in judgment was merely the logical outcome of the error the other person made.

You need to watch for this type of behavior. If someone tries to saddle you with more than your fair share of blame, call them on it, right then and there. And let your supervisor know. But the best approach is to be explicit about what you've done wrong. You don't say, "I should have returned all those calls rather than assume there was no problem." No, you say, "In retrospect, I see that the two calls from the purchasing manager probably spelled trouble, and I should have returned one of those alerts."

If need be, put it all in writing. Cite others who could vouch for the truth. Even if you had made an egregious error, don't let your feelings of vulnerability weaken your response if another worker or manager is trying to make you the sacrificial lamb. Fight back full bore.

The Lamest Excuse

Refusing to admit errors is bad enough. Offering the excuse that you're "only human, and humans make mistakes" is even worse. Only human? Being human is a good thing, not an excuse for mistakes. Aside from computers (which are a category unto themselves), humans are top of the line. Do not blame your wrong decisions or botched efforts on human frailty or fallibility. "I'm only human" suggests that you've let yourself off the hook before the other person even has a chance to consider what you've done. If they react unreasonably and refuse to forgive you for slipping up, then you can invoke your humanity as a reason for fair treatment, but never as an excuse. When employees tell me they're "only human" (and I've heard it plenty), I'm tempted to reply, "Well, to err is human. And to forgive is divine. But I'm only human too, so just get it right."

Keep Cool in a Crisis

In every office, the occasional crisis will hit. It could be a brief squall—say, your department needs to drastically modify an elaborate architectural design in two days, and three people are on vacation. Or it could be a larger and longer storm system—a former employee has thrown a sexual harassment suit at the company, and recriminations and counterrecriminations are thick in the air. Because most major disruptions at work tend to arise from personnel issues rather than from actual business problems, the level of emotionalism is often very high.

These are tricky and tough situations to navigate. It's very difficult not to "take sides" when there's a crisis that's splitting the workforce, and it's hard to stay focused on the work at hand when there's any sort of uproar. It seems to be a human trait to want to watch or get involved in altercations. The adrenaline level rises and people feel more alive, though not in a healthy way. In my years working for corporations, I found these crisis phases intriguing, and I could rarely just remain on the sideline as an observer. In fact, I used to seek them out. Until I learned the hard way that the best approach to workplace maelstroms is "do not get involved!" (This isn't always possible, of course; I provide strategies below for those situations in which you're involved whether you like it or not.)

Years ago, I might have suggested that you try to be the "eye of the storm," that you strive to be the one who "saves the day" by keeping your head clear as everyone else goes haywire. But that approach rarely works. Being in the middle of a storm, you're likely to get very wet. In political terms, this means that getting involved in major workplace conflicts, even if you're not a primary protagonist, can taint you. It's rare that you're going to come up with the solution that will "save the day." More likely, you'll waste time, energy, and political capital, and will have nothing to show for it except a learning experience. Few positive alliances at work are forged in the midst of crises, but plenty of lasting enmities are.

Cowardice is not acceptable, though. Stick up for what you think is right. If an ally of yours, a colleague you trust and respect, is being unfairly assailed, of course you should do what you can to help this person out. But that's not the same as making it your full-time cause. Resist the tendency to act as if any enemy of your friend is your enemy too. There are probably dynamics involved that have nothing to do with you, and about which you might not even know. So keep an even keel as you deal with everyone, regardless of what's happening behind the scenes.

Steer clear of major conflicts and give a wide berth to explosive situations. When and where there's actual yelling, don't even think about getting involved—don't even ask what's going on. Wait until the next day, when the smoke clears, to find out the grisly details. And be thankful that you don't have to deal with the situation up close.

How to Keep on an Even Keel

Unfortunately, you don't always have the option of sitting out a serious storm. Perhaps the situation involves you—a co-worker is angling for your job and has pulled a completely unacceptable maneuver that requires you to marshal all your allied forces. Or there's a massive shake-up at the company that has people in an uproar, with no one sure whether they'll have a job on any given Monday and backs being stabbed left and right. Maybe it's a nearly impossible project that has workers in a state of extreme agitation from overwork, inadequate sleep, and severely frayed nerves.

The range of causes is vast, but don't let the causes distract you from the immediate reality. What you're aiming for is—most important—to weather the crisis without sustaining significant damage at the workplace (or professionally, of course). That's priority number one. Along with that, you don't want your workdays to be a living hell for the duration of the office catastrophe, so finding some internal balance is critical too. The third concern is comporting yourself in a manner that will raise your stature at the company after the firestorm is doused or burns itself out.

Depending on how severe the situation is, self-preservation might be all that's possible, but frequently by maintaining a level head you can look good in comparison to most others and come off as a cool-headed professional rather than as a hysteric. If you follow the following guidelines, you'll have a solid foundation from which to cope with any office earthquake.

Remember that it's just a job. Because tempers flare so brightly in the face of deceit and other horrendous workplace behaviors, it's easy to lose perspective. In all likelihood, this isn't a matter of life and death; if the worst happens, you can find another job. If your reputation is tarnished, you'll find a way to restore it in the future. For perspective, hold up this situation against something far more traumatic in your mind.

Pay extra attention to maintaining your personal life. Many people carry workplace crises home with them and spend all their waking hours obsessing over what's going on at the office, which makes it worse and destroys perspective. See the drama as an opportunity not only to advance your standing but also to learn—about your company, about workplace dynamics, and about the character of the individuals which whom you work.

- ▶ Remember that everybody thinks they're right. No matter how despicably some workers and managers are behaving in your eyes, they can justify their actions. Few people ever admit to themselves that they're morally depraved. By acknowledging other players' sense of what's right, you can proceed more strategically than can someone who's focused exclusively on their own sense of reality.
- ▶ Breathe deep and apply the twenty-four-hour rule (from Chapter 5) as often as necessary. Employees

might be trying to get you going. For you, victory lies in not succumbing to rage or confusion. Don't let anyone else impose his or her state of mind on you.

▶ Even if you don't feel calm inside, maintain a composed demeanor. You give less away when your surface appears unruffled, and everyone notices and appreciates dignified behavior.

▶ Speak with utmost caution. Trust no one at work completely. "Drive defensively." Until you're sure of what's happening in a given place and moment, which is very difficult during a crisis, say no more than is necessary. But don't forget to distinguish between allies and foes; just don't place too much trust in an ally under stress.

▶ Treat even those you least trust with some basic decency. Don't ever turn your back on them, but don't descend to the level of refusing to say good morning.

▶ If people in the conflict start gravitating toward you, take this role and run with it. If you can maneuver yourself into being one of the main peacemakers you'll emerge with a lot of political power.

When You're on (an) Edge

If you're not immediately involved in a workplace fiasco, consider yourself lucky. But being on the periphery, you might find some opportunities to capitalize on the disorder. While you work to leverage the situation to your advantage, you need to be vigilant and not become more deeply embroiled in the crisis. Misery loves company, and frantic workers tend to pull bystanders into their conflicts. So beware of the human tendency to "rubberneck." Some people find workplace fiascoes at least as interesting as traffic accidents.

Don't play favorites from the sideline. Avoid conversations about the conflict. Once you start to discuss it with other people, your sympathies might be obvious.

If you see a power or performance vacuum has been created as attention and resources are being diverted to the flare-up, that's your opportunity. (It might be a simple move, such as taking over the writing of a periodic report.) Once you've taken on an activity, it's not easy for someone to wrest it back.

Articulate Your Ambitions

You've learned how to face the reality of the workplace, how to best interact with different echelons of workers and managers, how to use deft communication to influence outcomes, how to organize your time and space and information, and how to share credit graciously, accept blame painlessly, and steer clear of radioactive fallout. All these skills will help ensure that you prevail in the competitive work arena.

The last piece of the puzzle is knowing how to actively move ahead, how to expand your horizons, move up the ladder, and otherwise take control of your professional advancement. Of course, you can merely wait for things to fall into your lap—a promotion, sensational raise, or an offer to start a new office in Paris—or you can make things happen. I strongly encourage you to go the active route. Be proactive.

What's the best way to gain more responsibility and advance your career? It's very simple, actually: Ask for it.

---

way to go! Don't necessarily wait until you think you're due for a promotion. A sales representative had been at the pet supply firm for only two years and yet he was already a top performer. The regional manager had left soon after this person was hired, but that position had remained unfilled for nearly two years. There were five other salespeople in the company, and they all had a lot more years there than my acquaintance. Anyway, he decided to ask the CEO for the regional manager position. Even though he was a great performer, he was still "underqualified" in some ways for the slot. But he thought he could handle it. When the CEO heard the request, even though it seemed premature in some ways, a light went off. He realized that he hadn't filled the position because he didn't much care for the five other salespeople. And he thought the nerve my acquaintance demonstrated in asking for the job would make him a good manager. So he skipped over the five other potential candidates and awarded the job to the "newcomer."

Put Your Manager on Alert That You're Eager to Grow

Even if you don't think you're ready to advance to the next level, it's smart to express your ambitions. Managers are more likely to assign career-building projects and roles to those who've expressed a keen interest than those who quietly work away and hope the quality of their efforts will be rewarded. You do not want to be too pushy, of course, or the effect can be contrary to your wishes. Be attuned to your manager's style. Perhaps she's a supervisor who will say something once and expect people to pick up on it, for example. If so, she would not appreciate it if you harped on any subject, let alone your desire to take on more responsibility. But another manager might require repetition to get your point across. Play it carefully, but don't "play it safe."

This advice is most critical for those who are not inclined to step forward. I heard about a position opening up at a publishing company where a friend of mine works as an editor, so I encouraged her to apply for the spot. Her personality is fairly low-key, perhaps even a little timid, so it took a lot of urging on my part to get her to speak up. In fact, the job went to someone else, but several months later a different position unexpectedly opened up, and the division VP contacted my friend directly to apply. This time she got the job.

Don't Fear Reaching Beyond Your Means

One of the big secrets of life—especially at work—is that sometimes all it takes to attain a goal is the willingness to try. Take the pet supply salesman. He asked for a position for which he was technically underqualified. But by sending the signal that he had ambition, he instantly raised his qualification level.

You might have the same experience. All sorts of factors play a role, including luck and, perhaps most of all, personality. Or perhaps the company would prefer to promote you over a few old-timers because you'll settle for $18,000 less in salary. (Always go for the title, not the money, when you're young.)

IF IT DOESN'T EXIST, INVENT IT

Sometimes, unconventional approaches to career growth are the most powerful. For example, perhaps your company has no promotion opportunities available for you right now, but you see a need for a position that doesn't exist. So you might suggest that the company create this job (to be filled by you, naturally). By staking out uncharted territory, you're free to define your own parameters of influence.

Here's a perfect example: Jack was a junior marketing manager at a catalog company about five years ago. It was a comfortable situation, but there was no immediate growth potential. The company was doing fairly well, slow but steady growth; all the executives were fairly young (i.e., in their forties, which used to be considered reasonably young for executives!); operations ran smoothly; old-faithful marketing techniques still seemed to be pulling their weight.

Jack had always been enthusiastic about technology, and he made sure to read a lot of publications about computers, particularly business applications. So when the Web started to become commercialized in a big way, Jack was paying attention. What he did was to make a study of it, mostly in his spare time. His research included informal interviews with many people in the know, including some luminaries-to-be who were launching their own Web-based e-commerce companies. Within four months, Jack had created an elaborate presentation about the possibilities the Web offered his company—essentially, he'd prepared an intracompany business plan, in which he suggested he be appointed manager of Web marketing and given a modest budget. If it didn't pan out, he said, he would be happy to return to his previous duties. "Just give me six months."

His presentation went over well enough that he was put in charge of a research project, in which he was commissioned to find out exactly what the initial outlay would be, who the best vendors were, and so on. Early on, he had the company outfitted with a T1 line, and soon many of the company honchos started to pop into Jack's office on a near-daily basis. (He became adept at explaining things to them as he worked on-line—a skill few techies have mastered.) Within four months, the company launched its Web site, with Jack now in charge of his own three-person department and assuming a key strategic role. The executives had the foresight to heed Jack's advice that every marketing decision should take the Web strategy into account.

About two years ago, Jack was made executive VP of the company's Web division, and at the award banquet the CEO called Jack "the fiber-optic tail that wags the paper-catalog dog."

But don't lose sleep worrying over whether you can handle the job. Get the job first; figure out how you'll handle it after. It took brains to get where you are, so chances are you have what it takes to handle the next rung up. One way or another, you'll find a way if you want to. If you know you're not in the right place, for example, then you can keep on moving, especially once you've earned a higher title. When you find a niche you enjoy, where you'll be satisfied to spend a few years, then you can turn your energies to making up any shortfall in your qualifications—usually, all that's required is that you hire people with the expertise you lack.

Part of the game of getting ahead in business is to adopt a Machiavellian attitude of the ends justifying the means. What

THE PRINCIPLE THAT PETERED OUT

Some people cite the Peter Principle as a reason to take it slow in rising up the ladder. This idea, which was proposed in *The Peter Principle,* a best-selling book by an education professor published in the late 1960s, is that employees are promoted until they hit their level of incompetence, and that if you set your autopilot on "climb," you'll eventually reach a place of great personal and professional dissatisfaction. Well, satire is all well and good in its place, but as a guiding force this bogus "principle" is worthless.

I'm recommending isn't on the order of a medical technician posing as a brain surgeon. It's just business.

Basically, it's counterproductive thinking. If you really believe there's a Peter Principle, you'll never get ahead. If the idea ever did apply, it's obsolete now—the peeling away of middle management layers from corporate bureaucracies has left a lot less room for incompetent managers to tuck themselves in for the long haul.

What Will the Others Think?

Fear of what coworkers will think of them is the number one reason people hold back from taking risks inside their companies. "I couldn't possibly ask for that promotion; after all, there are three better-qualified people in our department." Really? Well, if they have any work intelligence, they'll all ask for that promotion as well—and may the best employee win. (Not the "most qualified," mind you, but "the best.")

I offer you my strongest advice here: Transcend embarrassment! Discard all of those stifling worries about "how it would look." Perhaps your coworkers will all say to each other "Some nerve!" when you ask for a promotion. Or maybe, when your colleagues witness your show of ambition, it will prompt them to do the same. That must not be your concern.

Your coworkers will get over it. More important, they're not the people you live with. Looking out for numero uno is your main responsibility. As I've been urging you all along, maintain that mental dividing line between work and the other, more important parts of your life, such as friends and family. It's the same advice I give to managers: Don't think of

HOW PROMOTIONS AND HIRES ARE REALLY MADE

The single most powerful word in the language with regard to being hired for excellent positions or getting a plum promotion is "chemistry." If two candidates are vying for the same job, and both are reasonably acceptable in terms of their credentials, the decision always comes down to personal chemistry—which one the hiring executive would prefer to work with on a daily basis. In fact, I've seen people hire the far less qualified candidate because they preferred the person's presence.

People either click or they don't. That's why the first impression is so incredibly important in business (and general life) situations. Candidates who fail to get hired for a top spot call me sometimes and

your coworkers (or subordinates) as friends. Camaraderie is nice, but self-care is key.

As my earlier example illustrates, there are many factors involved. A big one is personality. It's simple: Bosses prefer to promote people they can work with easily. The most qualified candidate is often also the most obnoxious, and this is a big reason positions remain unfilled for months or even years. I see it all the time. (At the same time, many companies do a terrible job of grooming and training their employees, and so they're averse to hiring from within. Familiarity seems to breed

whine, "Why didn't they hire me? Look at my Ivy League pedigree! Look at my track record!" I don't reply, however tempting it is, "Well, sure, but look at the smile the other, less hotshot candidate brings out in people, in contrast with the shudder you induce."

It helps immeasurably when you like the people you work with and who answer to you. (Not so that you relax your boundaries and forget to compartmentalize, but rather so you don't mind being around them all day five or six days a week.) This line of reasoning should be just as important to you in terms of accepting a job or a promotion. Never take a job where you really like the opportunity and it seems great but you hate the boss. Because rarely is the boss going away. And if it's a privately owned company, the owner is never going away.

contempt, and bosses often fail to realize how many strong, qualified candidates they have in their company.)

Yes, your colleagues may think you're a pushy, ruthless so-and-so when they see that you really go for it. That's the risk you take. But that's also the point of doing it: You want to get ahead, not mark time. All the methods and approaches I've described in these pages are intended to make your workdays crisis-free and smooth flowing. And the direction of that flow will be onward and upward, provided you take the calculated risks of asking for what you want.

So You Think You're Special?

Each category of employee could receive a chapter dedicated exclusively to their own work-related issues: women, African Americans, Jews, gays, the disabled, and so on. In a complex, highly pluralistic society such as ours, there's a tremendous amount to share and discuss. In fact, many issues that relate to a number of so-called special interests (i.e., the majority of the country) are covered in the earlier chapters. As a sendoff parcel, however, I'm singling out four prominent workplace constituencies for some special treatment.

Younger Workers

With a mighty economy, educated young workers have faced a very ingratiating work world. There are both good and bad aspects.

- ▶ The good: a sense of entitlement that makes it a snap for them to ask for hefty starting salaries, great benefits, and even informal working conditions. Many have a healthy irreverence. They're highly competitive, and eager to take on everything.
- ▶ The bad: a sense of entitlement that's unconnected to the need to work hard and strive. No awareness that they have very much to learn, and therefore they tend to be less inclined to ask questions. Too much irreverence without understanding what the value of workplace traditions might be. Hypercompetitiveness makes it hard for them to admit mistakes or share

credit; underdeveloped people skills; unwillingness to pay some dues.

► If economic difficulties start to kick in, the younger workers who will be most valuable (aside from computer programmers, because there's such a scarcity of them) will be those who know how to forge relationships and have mastered the people skills that still make the world go around.

► Suggestions: Seek out mentors to learn specifically those skills that are in short supply among the youth, such as general business knowledge and the finer points of communication.

► Resist the urge to talk without first considering the effect of your words. Focus on listening during the first phase of your career (say, the first year); you learn more that way. Learn to scope out the territory, to take the measure of the people around you, and to put some spin into everything you say.

Older Workers

► Even though the media exaggerates trends in order to keep people reading and watching, there are some real changes in the workplace that have increased insecurity among middle-aged workers. Instead of arriving at a greater sense of security as they age, they're facing more uncertainty and flux. The media present this as if it's a good thing, but few people are happy about not being sure their job will last or if they'll be replaced by a machine or a twenty-three-year-old.

► Don't despair or panic. You're not necessarily facing a

future of diminishing expectations and returns.
Remember that your experience in the world is
extremely valuable, that your understanding of business extends farther than the dot.com sphere. Countless companies will continue to value the skills,
shrewdness, knowledge, maturity, and wisdom that
older employees have in far greater measure than
younger ones.

► Appearance-wise: Stay youthful, without striving to
appear young. Find a balance—not fogey-ish but still
dignified.

► Do not be intimidated by computer technology,
because the more prowess you have the easier it will
be to adjust to new situations and to be treated with
respect by younger cohorts. There are still plenty of
executives in the world who don't have much to do
with computers or palm pilots, but people in their forties are certainly expected to be proficient in the use
of any of the office software they need for their job.
And many fifty-somethings have also gotten the
knack. If you feel you're behind the curve, consider
taking a class.

Temps

► Unless you have reasons that impel you to want to
remain on temp status, try to make the jump to full-
time. Receiving a fair benefits package alone should be
sufficient reason to make the leap.

► With a powerful economy creating a seller's market
for labor, this is a great time to go from temporary to

permanent worker status. Most temp agencies and
their clients have well-developed temp-to-perm
procedures.

▶ Scope out clients to see whether you think you would
want to work there. Be an "active shopper." If an
opportunity exists, then definitely go for it. Some
companies post listings at the site, others don't. If
there are no postings, you can even ask your boss at
the temp agency. It happens all the time—temps get
hired by clients. The client company will pay your
employer a fee if the deal works out.

Telecommuters

▶ Many people are finding telecommuting to be over-
rated. It's very isolating, and forcing yourself to work
when you could laze around all day is no mean feat
for a lot of people. Don't assume it's a cure-all for all
your anxieties and time-management problems,
because it introduces entirely new ones all its own.

▶ Telecommuters are off the political radar screen. Out
of sight, out of mind is the name of the game. So if
you want to advance at your company, don't telecommute. You need to be at the office, physically present
in the power circle, to get anywhere in the power
game. If you're not where the boss is, you're not going
to get that promotion.

▶ If you're a nonpolitical family person who wants to
minimize hassles (including the commute) and you
know you have the self-discipline to follow through
on whatever your plan of action is, then telecommut-

ing could be an excellent option. All others should give it a long look before taking the plunge. Another approach is to partially telecommute: Work at home only one or two days a week.

▶ Don't think you're going to accomplish all manner of household projects. Successful telecommuters treat their work time very much as they did in an office environment.

Summing Up:
How to Make It in the
Real World of Work

IT SEEMS ONLY APPROPRIATE TO CLOSE
this chapter—and hence the book—with a personal note. After all, the information and advice
in this book is personal. All the observations, an-
ecdotes, tactics, and strategies derive from my
twenty-plus years in the business world. As an
employee, executive, business owner, headhunter,
and now a broadcast journalist, I've had the advantage of seeing how people function (and dys-
function) on the job. As a recruiter, it's been part of
my mission to make a study of all things work-
related. I'd be surprised to encounter a personality
or workplace situation that I haven't seen already.

When I was just starting out in the work world, had someone told me—a somewhat shy teenager from a working-class background who attended a nonpedigree college—that I could achieve as much as I have, I wouldn't have believed it. My career so far has been pretty fabulous—varied, stimulating, lucrative, and high-powered. But above all, the reason I consider myself a success is that I'm truly happy doing what I do. To that insecure young man in Armonk, New York, all this would seem far-fetched at minimum. He thought profound success, career satisfaction, and renown were available only to the elite—the brilliant, the glamorous, and the already rich.

I'm glad to have found that such a belief was wrong. I don't consider myself an intellectual whiz, but I've been able to keep up with other, brainier types in the business world. In fact, some of the most intelligent people I've met have proven to be incapable of managing their work lives. It's well known now that high IQ and SAT scores do not necessarily presage great success in life, and that greatly successful men and women do not necessarily possess stellar gifts. Rather, it's the combination of guts, drive, and a good share of common sense that win the day.

I attribute my own success to following the ideas presented in this book—understanding that work is a game with its own coherent rules and learning how to play as effectively as I could. I've gone through the steps, cultivating alliances and other workplace relationships, maintaining a positive, enthusiastic attitude (most of the time), and playing the political angles. I organize my life to optimize work, making sure to balance labor and leisure, primarily by being timely in the first place, so I never have to recuperate from burnout or overstress.

I communicate in a direct manner, but make certain to be polite so people don't respond with excessive emotion. When I make a mistake, I acknowledge it, make amends if any are necessary, remind myself not to make that same error again, and move on. I pay close attention to how I communicate and how I handle my relationships with other professionals. Because these elements are the very heart and soul of working.

It seems odd to me that so many people struggle with such straightforward, nearly formulaic requirements. Perhaps the most obvious things are easiest to take for granted. Often when I conduct seminars about work life, audiences respond most powerfully to the simplest suggestions: always show up at work on time; don't argue with your boss; dress to fit in, not to stick out.

What I do not do is confuse work with the rest of life. I've always maintained a full social world beyond my corporate existence. And I'm not afraid to reach for the stars; even in my earliest employment phase, I was willing to ask for responsibilities that were technically beyond my abilities. Amusingly enough, I always managed to handle them once they were given to me. But I've never let fears over what others might think hold me back. At the same time, I've always carefully avoided revealing personal information that could be manipulated against me.

I've seen how powerful and valuable the program in this book can be. And I hope you take the advice to heart, and apply it thoroughly in your work life. And then write to me (stephen@viscusigroup.com) or call my radio show, "On the Job with Steve Viscusi" (1-877-562-6642), to share your success stories.

ACKNOWLEDGMENTS

It is impossible to write a book like this without the collaboration of many, many different people. I have asked hundreds of people to share their experiences and advice as I wrote this book, consulting those who have employed me as well as those who have been employed by me.

I am grateful to Mark Baven for his editorial insight, his way with words, and his help putting all the pieces of this book together. I also want to thank Lark Productions' Lisa DiMona, Karen Watts, Robin Dellabough, and Alice Wolfram, whose tireless efforts on my behalf made this book a reality, and Mark Hendricks, who first introduced me to Lark. Sarah Silbert, my editor at Three Rivers Press, has also been tremendously supportive in all of the ways an author hopes an editor will be.

My thanks go to Karla Swatek, a book publicist extraordinaire, who has also become a close friend. And hats off to David Hahn and Adrienne Hirsch of Planned Television Arts, the best book PR people around. I'm also grateful to Brian Belfiglio and his staff at Three Rivers Press. And thanks to all the people listed in the following paragraphs who have helped me make it in the real world of work, some of whom have been mentioned in the body of the book, most of whom have not:

My first real boss and mentor, Mr. Louis Euster, whose faith in me led me to the career path and life path I am on today. Through that job at Euster Associates, I was able to find role models, mentors, and friends who became part of this book. They include Addie Powell and Dan DeClerq, who were at the time sales reps at Knoll; my friends and coworkers from Euster Associates/The Modern Furniture Barn; fellow headhunter Richie Harris, who "recruited" me from

The Modern Furniture Barn; and Naomi Rosan, who became my first business partner.

Friend and mentor from the advertising world, Richard Presser of R. Presser and Associates. Linda Kline, who opened her doors and files to me when I first went into business.

My very early staff from The Viscusi Group, Inc.—they went through good times and bad with me, and they all deserve thanks. They include Jack Crimmins, Joy Kuhn, Lisa Zucker, Valerie Glod, Chris Stulpin, Sharon Peckham, Toni Riviello-DeRosa, and Tom Boland.

I'm deeply inspired by the memory of my dear friend, the late Brother James X. Collins, and all my friends from the De LaSalle Christian Brothers community and my many friends from Manhattan College.

From Haworth, I want to thank Mr. Jerry Haworth, Dick Haworth, and Jerry Johanneson. My former direct boss, Frank Baudo, and former Haworth executives Harvey Leopold and Judith Becker Thomas. Also within the furniture industry, I must thank former Steelcase executive Michelle Montminy; her husband, Joe Berasi; and current Steelcase executives Larry Leete, Dave Scherff, and Jeannie Bochette. KI CEO, Dick Resch, for believing in me and The Viscusi Group, Inc. Kimberly Christman, president of Pallas Textiles; Ron Kass, president of The Robert Allen Group, and his wife, Terry Keenan, of CNNfn. Knoll executives Liz Needle and Andrew Cogan and Herman Miller executives George Kordaris, Randy Kloostra, and Janet Minarik. The following furniture editors and publishers: Michael Wolf of *Monday Morning Quarterback* and his wife, Liz; Brad Powell of *Office Insight*; Mayer Rus, editor-in-chief, and Mark Strauss, publisher, of *Interior Design Magazine*; Katie Sosnowchik, editorial director, Martina Scanlan, publisher, and Beverly Russell, editor-at-large, of *Interior & Sources*. Julie Lasky, editor-in-chief of *Interiors* and former *Interiors* publisher, Dennis Cahill (who "discovered me"); and Roger Yee, editor, *B3*. Chris Kennedy of The Merchandise Mart, along with Mark Falanga, Mel

Schlitt, John Brennan, Kate Flaherty, Tricia Shelton, Monica DeBartolo, and Maria Avalos all deserve thanks. Karen Gustafson of The Gustafson Group PR firm, who has handled public relations for The Viscusi Group, Inc., for more than ten years. Liz Bruder and her husband, Ken Frydman, of the *New York Daily News,* who have been huge supporters. My friends and mentors: former Congressman Fred Richmond, Phil Scatturo of Allen & Company, and friend Robert W. Wilson. All have inspired me to think and grow rich. Sonny Joseph, whose penchant for work has been an inspiration, along with Andy Wolf, whose drive is contagious.

From the radio world, Ray White is my first thank-you for bringing me to Ben Manilla of Ben Manilla Productions, who introduced me to Bob Bruno, of WOR radio in New York City and Ken and Daria Dolan also of WOR. The Dolans let me into the studio and shared their craft. They deserve a huge thanks, as do Joan Hamburg and Arthur Schwarz of WOR, all of whom invited me onto their shows. Thanks to the prodding of Ed Walsh and Bob Bruno. It was Bob Bruno who got me my first job in radio at WVIP in Mt. Kisco, New York, with Mr. Martin Stone, who launched my first show. But that show would not have been possible without the help of Michael Harrison, publisher and editor of *Talkers* magazine; Valerie Geller of Geller Media; Walter Sabo, president of Sabo Media; and Holland Cooke of the Holland Cooke newsletter. More thanks to all who have lent an ear to my dozens of tapes: Bob Carey of Syndicated Solutions, Inc., who is the syndicator of "On the Job with Steve Viscusi," along with George Green; Marty Miller of Associated Broadcast Group; Mike Caccioppoli, my producer; John Mainelli, my creative producer consultant for "On the Job," and Tony Maciulis, my first producer, along with John Calabro, engineer. At SSI, thank-you to Matt Sullivan and Bob Appel. Gene Lindsay of WHNZ AM 1250 Radio in Tampa, Florida, deserves a thank-you for taking a chance on me.

I also want to thank fellow authors Harvey Mackay, Dr. Shere Hite, Dr. Adele Scheele, Carole Hyatt, and Kate Bohner, as well as

Annie Fisher from *Fortune,* Carol Kleiman from the *Chicago Tribune,* and Eve Tahmincioglu from the *New York Times.* My friend and neighbor, Patricia Luchsinger, of *The Today Show* and her patient husband, Gary Matsumoto, and Jeff Jayson of *Good Morning America.* Thanks also to Jeff Taylor, of Monster.com

I could not have written the book without the support of my loyal and dedicated employees from The Viscusi Group today. VPs in our New York office, Arlene Rush, who has been a longtime friend and colleague, along with Jane Morris, and my faithful assistant, Alma Karassavidis.

My family is too large to name everyone, but it is essential to say what an influence my large Italian-American family has been on my workplace values. All four of my grandparents were born in Italy and came to the United States in the early 1900s. I represent second-generation Italian immigrants. My mother's family of ten children were very ambitious, mostly entrepreneurs. My father's brothers and sisters were all goal oriented, and those aunts and uncles formed a lasting impression on me as to what work is about.

Finally, my immediate family. My late mother, Mildred Albanese Viscusi, whose constant support and belief in me while growing up always made me feel important. She taught me to believe I could accomplish anything and, most important, gave me the enthusiasm to work with people. My father, Fred, who continues to support me and whose tolerance and calm demeanor I wish I had more of. My cousin Laura Lanza, who was raised with my sister and me and whose work ethic has always been an inspiration. My sister, Laura, who has been the best sister in the world and is always there for me. My longtime friends Dr. Max Link, Russ Schriefer, Jim Blair, Graham Walsh, Susan and Jeffrey Petre, and Stephen Costigan. And very special thanks to Casey McNamara.

INDEX

ABOUT THE AUTHOR

STEPHEN VISCUSI is the host of the nationally syndicated radio talk show "On the Job with Steve Viscusi," which is heard throughout the United States and Canada. He appears regularly as a workplace expert and strategist on national broadcast television and radio programs, such as ABC's *Good Morning America*, and he is also a frequent guest speaker and lecturer at workplace-related events. He also writes the syndicated workplace column "On the Job."

Viscusi is the CEO of The Viscusi Group, Inc., an international search practice ranked as one of the top ten firms in New York City by Crain's New York Business. Former President Bill Clinton invited Viscusi to participate in the White House "Forum on Corporate Citizenship," along with a select group of other CEOs representing a broad range of America's industries.

Viscusi was born and raised in Armonk, New York, and now resides in Manhattan's Upper West Side.

Visit the Viscusi Group Web site at *www.viscusigroup.com.*

E-mail: *stephen@viscusi.com*
Office tel.: 212-595-3811
Fax: 212-595-9103

For more information, please contact Karen Gustafson, Gustafson PR, tel. 212-724-4444, fax: 212-799-4863, or e-mail: *group@gustafsonpr.com.*